Mastering F#

I0010585

A comprehensive and in-depth guide to writing functional programs using F#

Alfonso García-Caro Núñez
Suhaib Fahad

BIRMINGHAM - MUMBAI

Mastering F#

Copyright © 2016 Packt Publishing

All rights reserved. No part of this book may be reproduced, stored in a retrieval system, or transmitted in any form or by any means, without the prior written permission of the publisher, except in the case of brief quotations embedded in critical articles or reviews.

Every effort has been made in the preparation of this book to ensure the accuracy of the information presented. However, the information contained in this book is sold without warranty, either express or implied. Neither the authors, nor Packt Publishing, and its dealers and distributors will be held liable for any damages caused or alleged to be caused directly or indirectly by this book.

Packt Publishing has endeavored to provide trademark information about all of the companies and products mentioned in this book by the appropriate use of capitals. However, Packt Publishing cannot guarantee the accuracy of this information.

First published: November 2016

Production reference: 1251116

Published by Packt Publishing Ltd.
Livery Place
35 Livery Street
Birmingham
B3 2PB, UK.
ISBN 978-1-78439-343-4

www.packtpub.com

Credits

Authors

Alfonso García-Caro Núñez

Suhaib Fahad

Reviewer

Basel Wael Abu-Jamous

Commissioning Editor

Ashwin Nair

Acquisition Editor

Ajith Menon

Content Development Editor

Zeeyan Pinheiro

Technical Editor

Kunal Chaudhari

Copy Editor

Zainab Bootwala

Project Coordinator

Izzat Contractor

Proofreader

Safis Editing

Indexer

Tejal Daruwale Soni

Graphics

Jason Monteiro

Production Coordinator

Shraddha Falebhai

About the Authors

Alfonso García-Caro Núñez is a linguist who, in recent years, changed the study of natural languages by the practice of their programming counterparts. He currently focuses on JavaScript and .NET development and has worked on developing mobile, web, and desktop applications for several industries, such as video games, education, green energy, or digital performances. He is also an international speaker who has presented at several conferences around the globe. His admiration for both the thriving JavaScript ecosystem and functional programming with F# made him look for a way to bring together both worlds, leading to the creation of Fable, an F# to JavaScript compiler that is attracting lot of attention from the community, and integrates the power and elegance of F# with the hundreds of JavaScript tools and libraries available.

I would like to say a big thank you to all the members of the incredibly supportive and welcoming F# community. Since my first timid steps into functional programming, I have been always encouraged to give my opinion and contribute to the development of the ecosystem and the language itself. Features and tools are important, but it is openness and collaboration that really makes you proud to belong to a community. Neither this book nor anything else in my life would have been possible without the care and love of my family. I dedicate this as well as all my work to the women of my life: my mother, wife, and daughter.

Suhaib Fahad is an entrepreneur and is running a startup; he is also an expert F# programmer and enthusiast, using F# in various domains within the products that he is building. He is extremely passionate about developing in functional languages and loves to engage with developers of different communities. He has also been researching and working with cloud scale applications since 2012. Fahad lives in Bangalore, the IT hub of India, with his wife and baby boy.

About the Reviewer

Dr Basel Abu-Jamous is a post-doctorate researcher in the area of bioinformatics at the University of Oxford. He is interested in the development of new computational algorithms that address bioinformatic questions with a special focus on tunable consensus clustering methods. He is also interested in the application of such methods in biology and medicine. For instance, he currently works in Dr. Steven Kelly's laboratory within the C4 Rice Project that aims to improve photosynthetic efficiency in rice and thus to enhance crop yields. As such, the C4 Rice Project is one of the scientific Grand Challenges of the 21st century, involving the coordinated efforts of researchers from 12 institutions in eight countries.

Previously, while being in the group of Professor Asoke Nandi at Brunel University London, he worked closely with Professor David Roberts, the Professor of Hematology at John Radcliffe Hospital and the University of Oxford, to understand the genetic programs responsible for erythropoiesis, that is, the production of red blood cells in human bodies. He was also in collaboration with Professor Adrian Harris and Professor Francesca Buffa, experts in breast cancer at Churchill Hospital and the University of Oxford, to analyze genetic regulatory pathways in breast cancer tumors under hypoxia, that is, low levels of oxygen. Additionally, he was also involved in the analysis of data from other areas including baker's yeast, malaria, and *E. coli* bacteria.

Dr Abu-Jamous received his Ph.D. from Brunel University London in July 2015 and was awarded the Dean's Prize for Innovation and Impact in Doctoral Research in the area of electronic and computer engineering in December of the same year. In January 2015, he was appointed by Professor Nandi as a research assistant at Brunel University London, and in July 2016 he moved to the University of Oxford.

He has published eight journal papers, fourteen peer-reviewed full-length papers in international conferences, and a research monograph book (Abu-Jamous, Fa, and Nandi, *Integrative cluster analysis in bioinformatics*, John Wiley & Sons, 2015).

Dr Abu-Jamous would like to thank the C4 Rice Project for funding his current research, Brunel University London and the UK National Institute for Health Research (NIHR) for funding his Ph.D. degree and his previous post-doctorate research (NIHR grant reference number RP-PG-0310-1004). He would also like to thank his current and previous supervisors, Dr Steven Kelly and Professor Nandi, respectively, and all colleagues, collaborators, friends, and family for their support.

www.PacktPub.com

For support files and downloads related to your book, please visit www.PacktPub.com.

Did you know that Packt offers eBook versions of every book published, with PDF and ePub files available? You can upgrade to the eBook version at www.PacktPub.com and as a print book customer, you are entitled to a discount on the eBook copy. Get in touch with us at service@packtpub.com for more details.

At www.PacktPub.com, you can also read a collection of free technical articles, sign up for a range of free newsletters and receive exclusive discounts and offers on Packt books and eBooks.

https://www.packtpub.com/mapt

Get the most in-demand software skills with Mapt. Mapt gives you full access to all Packt books and video courses, as well as industry-leading tools to help you plan your personal development and advance your career.

Why subscribe?

- Fully searchable across every book published by Packt
- Copy and paste, print, and bookmark content
- On demand and accessible via a web browser

Table of Contents

Preface

F# is a multiparadigm programming language that encompasses object-oriented, imperative, and functional programming language properties. Now adopted in a wide range of application areas and supported both by industry-leading companies who provide professional tools and by an active open community, F# is rapidly gaining popularity as it emerges in digital music advertising and creating music focused ads for Spotify, Pandora, Shazam, and anywhere on the web.

What this book covers

Chapter 1, *Getting Started with F#*, explains how to get started with F# with Visual Studio. A Simple hello world program is created and details about the project structure and file ordering and the differences between F# and C# in terms of usage are discussed.

Chapter 2, *Functional Core with F#*, teaches you about the functional core of F#, such as data types, type declarations, immutability, strong type interference, pattern matching, records, F# data structures, sequence expressions, lazy evaluation, making side effects explicit, and so on.

Chapter 3, *Data Structures in F#*, helps you understand how to use the available data structures in F# and write some basic custom data structures.

Chapter 4, *Imperative Programming in F#*, teaches you how to use control structures, more idiomatic .NET with F#, and interfacing with C# and generics.

Chapter 5, *Asynchronous Programming*, goes through the asynchronous programming model in F#, with a bit of cross-referencing or comparison drawn with the C# world.

Chapter 6, *Type Providers*, talks about some of the most common type providers, and additionally, also looks at the Query build that will help write LINQ-like queries for our custom collections.

Chapter 7, *Web Programming in F#*, teaches you how to build web servers using some of the most common .NET libraries as well as how you can write code for the browser in F# using WebSharper or Fable.

Chapter 8, *Application Development in F#*, explains how to write cross-platform desktop applications in F# using Fable and the Github Electron project.

Chapter 9, *Testing in F#*, teaches you how to write unit tests in F# with popular tools, and the advantages the language offers for this.

Chapter 10, *Distributed Programming in F#*, delves into using F# to implement the actor model popularized by Erlang, in order to write more robust software using decoupled actors that can run on different machines over a network and heal themselves in the eventuality of failure.

What you need for this book

All you need for this book is a computer that can comfortably run the following software applications: An F# IDE like Visual Studio 2015 (with Visual F# Power Tools), Visual Studio for Mac or Visual Studio Code with the Ionide extension.

Who this book is for

If you are a C# developer with a basic knowledge of F# and want to explore the functional programming paradigm further to master your F# skills, then this book is for you.

Conventions

In this book, you will find a number of text styles that distinguish between different kinds of information. Here are some examples of these styles and an explanation of their meaning.

Code words in text, database table names, folder names, filenames, file extensions, pathnames, dummy URLs, user input, and Twitter handles are shown as follows: "The class overrides a `ToString` function from the base class."

A block of code is set as follows:

```
let x = 20
    if not (x < 10) then
        printfn "x is greater than 10"
```

Any command-line input or output is written as follows:

```
> let p = new Point(10, 20);;
val p : Point = Point 10, 20
```

New terms and **important words** are shown in bold.

Warnings or important notes appear in a box like this.

 Tips and tricks appear like this.

Reader feedback

Feedback from our readers is always welcome. Let us know what you think about this book-what you liked or disliked. Reader feedback is important for us as it helps us develop titles that you will really get the most out of. To send us general feedback, simply e-mail feedback@packtpub.com, and mention the book's title in the subject of your message. If there is a topic that you have expertise in and you are interested in either writing or contributing to a book, see our author guide at www.packtpub.com/authors.

Customer support

Now that you are the proud owner of a Packt book, we have a number of things to help you to get the most from your purchase.

Downloading the example code

You can download the example code files for this book from your account at http://www.packtpub.com. If you purchased this book elsewhere, you can visit http://www.packtpub.com/support and register to have the files e-mailed directly to you.

You can download the code files by following these steps:

1. Log in or register to our website using your e-mail address and password.
2. Hover the mouse pointer on the **SUPPORT** tab at the top.
3. Click on **Code Downloads & Errata**.
4. Enter the name of the book in the **Search** box.
5. Select the book for which you're looking to download the code files.
6. Choose from the drop-down menu where you purchased this book from.
7. Click on **Code Download**.

Once the file is downloaded, please make sure that you unzip or extract the folder using the latest version of:

- WinRAR / 7-Zip for Windows
- Zipeg / iZip / UnRarX for Mac
- 7-Zip / PeaZip for Linux

The code bundle for the book is also hosted on GitHub at `https://github.com/PacktPublishing/Mastering-FSharp`. We also have other code bundles from our rich catalog of books and videos available at `https://github.com/PacktPublishing/`. Check them out!

Errata

Although we have taken every care to ensure the accuracy of our content, mistakes do happen. If you find a mistake in one of our books-maybe a mistake in the text or the code-we would be grateful if you could report this to us. By doing so, you can save other readers from frustration and help us improve subsequent versions of this book. If you find any errata, please report them by visiting `http://www.packtpub.com/submit-errata`, selecting your book, clicking on the **Errata Submission Form** link, and entering the details of your errata. Once your errata are verified, your submission will be accepted and the errata will be uploaded to our website or added to any list of existing errata under the Errata section of that title.

To view the previously submitted errata, go to `https://www.packtpub.com/books/content/support` and enter the name of the book in the search field. The required information will appear under the **Errata** section.

Piracy

Piracy of copyrighted material on the Internet is an ongoing problem across all media. At Packt, we take the protection of our copyright and licenses very seriously. If you come across any illegal copies of our works in any form on the Internet, please provide us with the location address or website name immediately so that we can pursue a remedy.

Please contact us at `copyright@packtpub.com` with a link to the suspected pirated material.

We appreciate your help in protecting our authors and our ability to bring you valuable content.

Questions

If you have a problem with any aspect of this book, you can contact us at questions@packtpub.com, and we will do our best to address the problem.

1
Getting Started in F#

F# is a functional first language in the .NET family and is a derivative of the **Meta-Language** (**ML**) family of languages. It shares many features with dialects of ML, which originally derives from the classical ML language designed by Robin Milner in 1973 at the University of Edinburgh. As a .NET language, F# code compiles to **Microsoft Intermediate Language** (**MSIL**), which runs on top of **Common Language Runtime** (**CLR**).

In this chapter, we will cover the following topics:

- The key features of F#
- The functional and imperative languages
- Using F# with Visual Studio
- Basic expressions in F#

Key features of F#

The following are some points that Distinguish the F# language from other .NET languages:

- F# is a functional first language, which means that functions are treated as first-class citizens, but it also provides ways to work with other paradigms, such as **object-oriented programming** (**OOP**) (as in C#).
- Unlike other languages, such as C#, which mixes expressions (language constructs returning a value) and statements (constructs that don't return a value), F# is an expression-based language. You can think of every syntax construct in F# as a small function.

- F# is a strongly-typed language, meaning that the type of every expression in the program is determined at compile time. This allows the compiler to make verifications in our code and enables great tooling support, such as autocompletion, refactoring, and so on.

- Additionally, F# has a very strong type inference mechanism to infer types for the expressions in a program. This removes much of the verbosity usually associated with strongly-typed languages.

- The .NET generics' type system is baked into the core of F#. For example, the programmer doesn't have to specify the functions to be generic; if the F# type system infers the variables can be generic (provided it is implemented that way), the function becomes generic. This makes it easier to write polymorphic code, that is, functions that can be reused with different types.

- F# has a module system that allows data structures to be specified and defined abstractly. Unlike C# namespaces, F# modules can contain functions that help you separate data (types) from logic (functions in modules).

- F# implements a pattern matching mechanism, which allows controlling conditions based upon structural similarities; whereas, other languages only allow value matching as in `IF...ELSE` statements in C#.

Functional and imperative languages

Imperative languages usually modify the state of a variable for most operations. This makes it more difficult to reason about our program, particularly when different parts of our code change values that are globally accessible. When a piece of code modifies a value outside its scope, we talk about side-effects (this may also include other state modifications, such as file or console operations). OOP tries to tame side-effects by *encapsulating* state. However, this is not always a complete solution, as objects often develop tight and complex dependencies with each other that are still difficult to reason with.

Functional languages solve this problem using pure functions. Pure functions are closer to the mathematical ideal of functions, in the sense that they don't have side-effects (don't change state outside their scope) and always produce the same output given the same input. Pure functions are easier to refactor and reason with because their output is predictable, and can be used as building blocks to write large programs with different techniques of function composition.

F#, as described, is a functional-first language, but the language can also deal with unavoidable side-effects such as file or logging operations.

To compare F# with a more imperative language, we can take the example of a Fibonacci sequence generator, as follows:

<table>
<tr>
<td>

```
public static int Fibonacci(int n)
{
    int a = 0;
    int b = 1;
    // In N steps compute Fibonacci sequence
iteratively.
    for (int i = 0; i < n; i++)
        {
            int temp = a;
            a = b;
            b = temp + b;
        }

        return a;
}
```

</td>
<td>

```
let rec fib n =
if n < 2
then 1
else fib (n - 2) + fib
(n - 1)
```

</td>
</tr>
</table>

For illustration purposes, C# in procedural style is used. It is also capable of more functional implementations, such as **Language Integrated Query** (**LINQ**). Also, performance is not taken into consideration.

In an imperative language, the algorithm is normally implemented as a loop, and progress is made by modifying the state of the variables used in the loop.

In F#, the Fibonacci sequence is implemented using recursion. The `let` keyword, which defines the function, and the `rec` keyword, which specifies the function, can be called recursively. Using recursion, we are *parameterizing* the state (we will pass the updated values as parameters to the next call) so we do not need to use mutable variables.

However, please note that programs exclusively using a functional style can have performance problems. In this book, we will take an intermediate approach of using imperative code when necessary.

F# and integrated development environments

F# is very well integrated into Visual Studio 2010 and higher versions. This is a first-class language along with C# and VB.NET. There is also support for F# in cross-platform **integrated development environments** (**IDEs**) such as Xamarin Studio, the Ionide extension for Visual Studio Code, or Atom. See http://fsharp.org/ for more information.

Using F# with Visual Studio

Visual Studio includes the default project templates for F#. We can look for **Visual F#** and see a list of templates available.

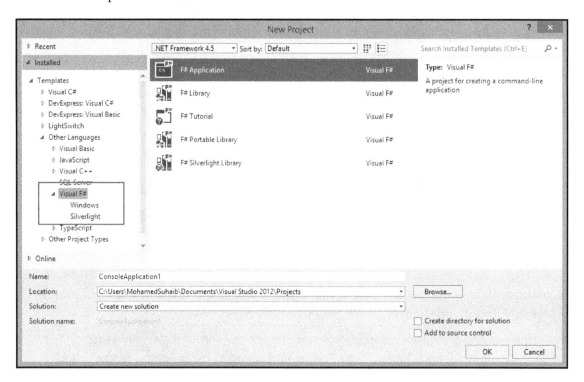

 The screenshots in this book have been taken with Visual Studio 2012, but they should be very similar to other Visual Studio versions.

For example, let's create an F# console application called `FSharpHelloWorld` and understand the different aspects of an F# project. The **Solution Explorer** lists the following files:

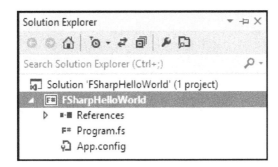

Open `Program.fs` and view the contents; it has very low-ceremony code to run the console application, which is as follows:

```
[<EntryPoint>]
let main argv =
    printfn "%A" argv
    0 // return an integer exit code
```

If you are a C# developer, some elements of this little program may surprise you. For example, the `EntryPoint` attribute indicates which function must be run when a console application starts. Also, as mentioned in the preceding code snippet, every expression in F# returns a value, so there is no need for an explicit `return` keyword.

Modify the `printfn` statement to include `"Hello World"`, as shown in the following code snippet:

```
[<EntryPoint>]
let main argv =
    printfn "Hello from F# :)"
    0 // return an integer exit code
```

F# project structure

F# projects follow a top-to-bottom structuring of program files. Unlike C# or VB.NET, this is the very first thing to understand to organize files and folders with F#.

 Folder management is not available in F# within Visual Studio by default; you will need to install the **Visual F# Power Tools** extension for that.

You will learn by adding some files to the hello world project, as follows:

- Add a new F# Employee.fs source file to the hello world project
- The Employee.fs file gets added to the end of the project
- Press *ALT* + the up arrow, or right-click and move up or down, to arrange the file as shown in the following screenshot:

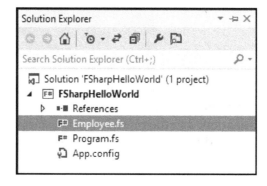

F# Script File

With F#, you can not write projects (.fsproj) containing module files (.fs), but also scripts (.fsx). These are single-file projects that are useful to write short programs, automation tasks, and so on.

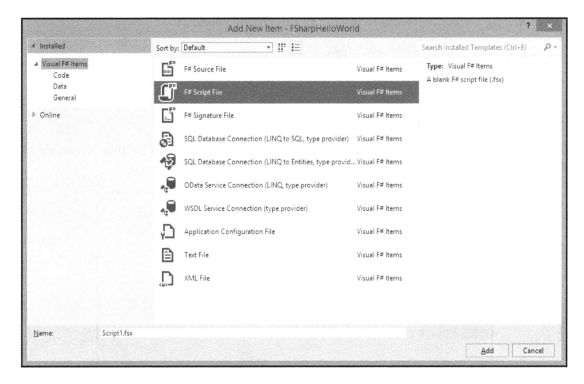

With **F# Script File**, we will get the following features:

- Full IntelliSense support
- Loading external files or .NET libraries
- Prototyping code that can easily be moved to a real codebase with minimal or no code changes
- An F# interactive window in Visual Studio that can be used to quickly test parts of the code from your F# script or normal F# files

Using the F# Interactive window

The **F# Interactive** window provides a **read-evaluate-print-loop** (**REPL**) to evaluate your expressions without having to create, build, and run an F# project. This is very useful for developers to work in *exploratory* mode.

The following are the two ways to use the **F# Interactive** window:

- Visual Studio
- Command line

The Visual Studio interactive window

To access the **F# Interactive** window from the menu, navigate to **View** | **Other Windows** | **F# Interactive**.

```
F# Interactive                                                    ▾ ☐ ✕

Microsoft (R) F# Interactive version 11.0.60610.1
Copyright (c) Microsoft Corporation. All Rights Reserved.

For help type #help;;

> |
```

 To evaluate an expression directly in the interactive window, terminate the code with double semicolons (; ;). This is not necessary in the F# source code.

Use the F# script files to quickly check a piece of code. We will now check this feature by writing a square root and a Fibonacci function. Add the following functions to a script file:

```
let sqr x = x * x
let rec fib n =
    if n < 2 then 1
    else fib (n - 2) + fib (n - 1)
```

After adding the preceding code snippet in the script file, perform the following steps:

1. Right-click on the selected code and select **Execute In Interactive** or press *Alt + Enter*.

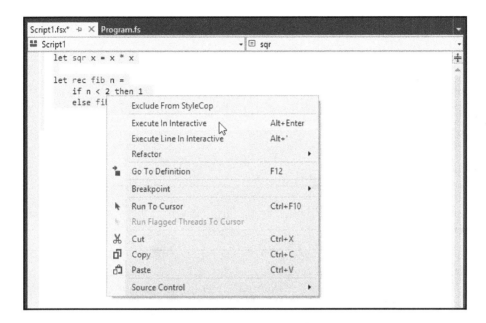

2. This will send the functions to the **F# Interactive** window. The window then displays the signature of the functions. Note that the syntax for signatures is a bit different from what we saw before. In this case, it means both functions accept and return an `int` value.

3. We can call the functions directly in the interactive window by applying an `int` argument to the name of the function, as shown in the following screenshot:

```
F# Interactive                                                          ▾ ☐ ✕

Microsoft (R) F# Interactive version 11.0.60610.1
Copyright (c) Microsoft Corporation. All Rights Reserved.

For help type #help;;

>

val sqr : x:int -> int
val fib : n:int -> int

> sqr 10;;
val it : int = 100
> fib 10;;
val it : int = 89
> |
```

There are some idioms that you will need to be familiar with when using **F# Script File** or the **F# Interactive** mode.

Idioms	Description

`#load`	This loads a script/F# file. For example, refer to the following piece of code:
	`#load "sample.fs"`
	`#load "sample.fsx"`

`#I`	This refers to a folder to load the assemblies in. For example, refer to the following piece of code: `#I @"C:\Program Files   (x86)\Reference Assemblies\Microsoft\Framework\.NETFramework\v4.0"`

`#r`	This refers to the assembly to load from the referenced folder. Usually, this is used in conjunction with #I.
	For example, refer to the following piece of code:
	`#I @"C:\Program Files   (x86)\Reference Assemblies\Microsoft\Framework\.NETFramework\v4.0"`
	`#r "presentationcore.dll"`

`#help`	This displays information about available directives.
`#quit`	This terminates the interactive session.
`#time [on / off]`	The #time directive toggles whether to display performance information or not. When it is enabled, F# measures real-time, CPU time, and garbage collection information for each session of code that is interpreted and executed.

The FSI interactive window

FSI interactive shell is a simple console app that is bundled with the F# installation. To open FSI, perform the following steps:

1. Open a terminal window.
2. Type `fsi` to log in to the FSI session.
3. Try some simple code to evaluate.

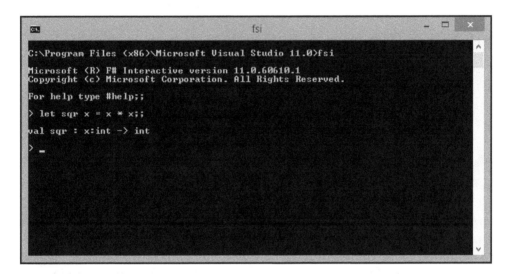

 In non-Windows platforms, the command to start the F# interactive session is `fsharpi`.

When you see code preceded by > in this book, it means that the line is supposed to be evaluated directly in an F# interactive session.

Basic values

In F#, every valid value must have a type, and a value of one type may not be bound to a value of another type. We will declare values in F# using the `let` keyword. For example, refer to the following piece of code:

```
// variable expression
let x = 10
// function expression
let add a b = a + b
```

As you learn F#, you will initially spend a lot of time getting the F# type checker to accept your programs. Being patient and analyzing the results with the F# type checker eventually helps you program better; you will later realize that the type checker is your best friend. Some rules about type checking are as follows:

- Every expression has exactly one type
- When an expression is evaluated, one of the following two things can happen:
  - It could evaluate to a value of the same type as the expression
  - It may raise an exception or error (this is actually a side-effect)

The `let` bindings can also be nested as follows:

```
let z =
    let x = 3
    let y = 4
    x + y
```

 Note that the inner `let` bindings are placed to the right of the outer `let` bindings. This is important because the F# compiler determines scope by indentation.

When an expression is bound to a value in a `let` binding, the value can be used within the body of `let` (its scope). If a value with the same name was declared previously, the previous definition is overridden with the new definition; this is called *shadowing* and is often used in F# instead of value mutation. Let's consider the following example:

```
let test () =
    let x = 5
    do
        let x = 10
        printfn "%i" x // prints 10
    x // returns 5
```

Here, we are not reassigning 10 to the previously declared x value. Instead, we are effectively creating a new value, as you can see, because in the outer scope x is still 5.

If needed, it is still possible to modify values in F#. For that, we will need to use the `mutable` keyword, as shown in the following piece of code:

```
let test() =
    let mutable x = 5
    do
        x <- 10 // assignment
        printfn "%i" x // prints 10
    x // returns 10
```

Getting started with functions

Anonymous functions, or lambdas, are defined with the `fun` keyword, followed by a sequence of parameters with the -> separator, and then the body of the function expression. The following is an example function to add two numbers:

```
> let sum = fun a b -> a + b;;
val sum : a:int -> b:int -> int
```

A shortcut for the preceding code is `let sum a b = a + b`.

The type for `sum` is `int -> int -> int`. Like other functional languages, this means that arguments are *curried*. Think of `sum` as a function returning another function, which can be partially applied, as we will see in the following section.

Partially applied functions

In F#, and other similar functional languages, functions actually have only one input and output. When we declare a function with multiple arguments, we are actually building functions that return other functions until the desired output is obtained. In the following code snippet, the two functions are effectively identical:

```
> let sum = fun x y z -> x + y + z;;
val sum : x:int -> y:int -> z:int -> int
> let sum' = fun x -> fun y -> fun z -> x + y + z;;
val sum' : x:int -> y:int -> z:int -> int
```

The apostrophe is a valid character in F# and it is often used to mark values with a slight modification from a previously existing one.

The application of lesser arguments than the arity (the total number of arguments a function can accept) is called a partial application.

```
> let sum a b = a + b;;
> let incr_by_ten = sum 10;;
> incr_by_ten 5;;
val it : int = 15
```

Partial functions also help in writing concise code with F# pipeline operators, as shown in the following code:

```
let res1 = List.map (fun x -> x + x) [2; 4; 6]
let res2 = List.filter (fun x -> x > 5) res1
```

The preceding code can be rewritten in a more expressive way using the pipe (| >) operator:

```
[2; 4; 6] |> List.map (fun x -> x + x) |> List.filter (fun x -> x > 5)
```

In F#, infix operators can be declared the same way as functions; the only difference is that we will surround them with parentheses in the declaration (for example, `let (++) x y = (x + y) * 2`) and then use them in the middle of the arguments (for example, `5 ++ 3`).

For C# and VB.NET users, this is much like the continuation style programming with LINQ functions. In LINQ, you will normally pipeline a sequence of function calls, as follows:

```
var listOfItems = someItems.Select(x => x.Name).OrderBy(x => x);
```

However, for this the type returned by the first method needs to implement the method we want to call next. This is not a limitation when using the pipe operator.

It is also possible to declare functions in a more similar way to languages such as C# (for example, `let sum (x, y) = x + y`), but there is an important difference-these functions take a *single tuple* argument. We will discuss tuples in `Chapter 2`, *Functional Core with F#*.

Recursive functions

In functional languages, recursion is used to express repetition or looping. For example, the Fibonacci sequence generator can be written as follows:

```
let rec fib n =
    if n < 2 then 1
    else fib (n - 2) + fib (n - 1)
```

We use the `rec` keyword to define a function as recursive. This is necessary to help the F# type checker infer the types of the function signature.

Every time a function is called recursively, a new routine is added to the call stack. As the call stack is limited, we must be careful not to overflow it. To prevent this, the compiler of F# and most functional programming languages implements an optimization called tail-call, which basically compiles down to a `while` loop. To enable this optimization, we will need to make sure the recursive call is the last expression in the function.

```
// tail-recursion
let factorial x =
    // Keep track of both x and an accumulator value (acc)
    let rec tailRecursiveFactorial x acc =
        if x <= 1 then
            // use the accumulator that has the final result
            acc
        else
            // pass the accumulator + original value again to the
recursive method
            tailRecursiveFactorial (x - 1) (acc * x)
    tailRecursiveFactorial x 1
```

Higher-order functions

As functions are first-class citizens in functional languages, we can pass them as arguments to other functions. When a function takes another function as an argument, we it a higher-order function. Let's consider the following example:

```
> let apply x f = f x
val map : x:'a -> f:('a -> 'b) -> 'b
> let sqr x = x * x
val sqr : x:int -> int
> let f = apply 5 sqr;;
val f : int = 25
```

The preceding code snippets perform the following functions:

- The `apply` function takes a function as a parameter and evaluates the function
- We will declare a `sqr` function, which squares an `int` value
- We will then call the `sqr` function through `apply`

Higher-order functions are very important to write composable and reusable code. Earlier, we saw `List.map`. Many of the functions in the `Collections` modules (`List`, `Array`, and `Seq`) accept functions as arguments so we can adapt their behavior to our needs.

Summary

In this chapter, we covered the basics of working with F# projects and used the interactive window to try out some basic constructs. Also, we saw a brief overview of different programming paradigms and the advantages of functional programming. In the next chapter, we will delve into some of the more powerful features of F#, such as record and union types as well as pattern matching.

2
Functional Core with F#

As we have seen, F# is a functional-first language where we create functions and apply them. The result of the evaluation of one of these expressions is a value, and the execution of the program is the evaluation of all the expressions that comprise it.

In this chapter, we will cover the following topics:

- F# types such as primitives, tuples, records, and unions
- Pattern matching
- Equality and comparison
- Reference cells and mutability

F# primitive types

The data types defined in F# are mapped directly with CLR. The following table defines the F# primitive types:

Name	F# type	Suffix	Example
Boolean	`bool`		`true/false`
Character	`char`		`'A'`
Text string	`string`		`"Hello World!"`
Short	`int16`	`s`	`15s`
Unsigned short	`uint16`	`us`	`100us`
Integer	`int`	(none)	`123`
Float/ Double	`float`	(optional) e	`2.,1.01,1.10e10`

Unsigned integer	`uint32`	u	`123u`
Long	`int64`	L	`9999L`
Unsigned long	`uint64`	UL	`9999UL`
Single	`float32` or `single`	f, (optional) e	`1.0f, 1.01f, 1.01e10f`
Decimal	`decimal`	m	`123m`
Big integer	`bigint`	I	`123I`
Signed byte	`sbyte`	y	`3y`
Unsigned byte	`byte`	uy	`5uy`
Native integer	`nativeint`	n	`123n`
Unsigned native integer	`unnativeint`	un	`123un`

The unit type

The `unit` type is used to indicate the absence of a specific value, but formally describes a set that possesses only a single element denoted by `()`.

```
>();;
val it : unit()
```

This value is often used in imperative programs. Functions returning `unit` simulate `void` methods in C# and VB languages.

Operator precedence

The precedence of operators in basic types is listed in increasing order.

Operator	Associativity
`or, ||, &, &&`	Left
`< op, > op,	op, & op`	Left
`&&&, |||, ^^^, ~~~, <<<, >>>`	Left
`^ op, ::, ->, :=`	Right
`as, when, ;`	Right

Custom operators

Operators are just functions in F#, and you can define a custom operator as if you are defining a function. The main differences are: you must surround the operator with parentheses in the definition and, in the case of infix operators, you can put the operator between two arguments.

F# allows creating new operators out of a sequence of certain characters. The allowed operator characters are !, %, &, *, +, −, ., /, <, =, >, ?, @, ^, |, and ~. Depending upon the exact character sequence, your operator will have a certain precedence and associativity. An example is shown in the following code snippet:

```
open System.Text.RegularExpressions
let (=~) input pattern = Regex.IsMatch(input, pattern)
// val ( =~ ) : input:string -> pattern:string -> bool
"some input" =~ ".*input"
// val it : bool = true
```

 The operator precedence is determined by the first character only.

Immutability, type declarations, and strong type inference

F# strongly adheres to immutability, meaning that the values declared in the program cannot be modified once they are constructed. Immutability also makes the code more readable because updates in the program state are more visible; thus it is easier to detect which operations affect the state. There are also F#-specific types, such as tuples, records, discriminated unions, and option types, which are immutable in their nature. They exhibit the following characteristics:

- Being immutable
- Values cannot be null
- Built-in structural equality and comparison

F# has pattern matching as a special feature (from the ML family). We will go through pattern matching over predefined types and then discuss the different structural types and how to construct values with them. In further chapters, we will take a look at all the F#-specific types and ways to declare and use them.

Pattern matching

Pattern matching is defined by a match expression, which has the following syntax:

```
match expression with
| pattern1 -> expression1
| pattern2 -> expression2
|...
|...
| patternN -> expressionN
```

When a match expression is evaluated, the expression to be matched is first evaluated, and its value is compared with the listed patterns in order. The evaluation will stop after the first match.

The simplest form of pattern matching resembles the well-known `switch` statement from other languages and compares a value against a list of constants or patterns. For example, the Fibonacci sequence can be defined succinctly using pattern matching, as follows:

```
let rec fib2 n =
    match n with
    | 0 -> 0
    | 1 -> 1
    | x -> fib2 (x - 2) + fib2 (x - 1)
> fib2 10;;
val it : int = 55
```

 Note that, unlike `switch`, the pattern matching expression returns a value.

Now, we will see more advanced uses of pattern matching.

Functions with pattern matching

We can use the `function` keyword to declare more succinctly a function whose body is a pattern matching expression. The same Fibonacci sequence can be defined as follows:

```
let rec fib2 = function
    | 0 -> 0
    | 1 -> 1
    | x -> fib2 (x - 2) + fib2 (x - 1)
```

We will also omit the last argument (here, the single argument), which is directly fed to the pattern matching expression.

Pattern expressions

The vertical bar, |, can be used to define a choice in the pattern. We can further write the Fibonacci sequence in a shorter way, which is as follows:

```
let rec fib2 = function
    | 0 | 1 as x -> x
    | x -> fib2 (x - 2) + fib2 (x - 1)
```

We will use the as keyword to project the value matching the (0 | 1) choice into a variable.

Guard expressions

Patterns can also be qualified with a predicate using the when keyword (guard expressions). The expression is evaluated within the context of the pattern. Again, we can modify our Fibonacci sequence as follows:

```
let rec fib2 n =
    match n with
    | x when x < 2 -> x
    | x -> fib2 (x - 2) + fib2 (x - 1)
```

Incomplete matches

If the match expression doesn't include patterns for all use-cases, then the F# compiler generates a warning as the program will fail if no pattern matches a given expression. This forces the developer to list all cases exhaustively, and it is a clear advantage over the traditional switch or if...else statements.

Wildcard pattern

The _ symbol matches all possible values. It is called wildcard pattern.

```
let is_even x =
    match x with
```

```
| i when i % 2 = 0 -> true
| _                -> false
```

This is useful to write a pattern for complex types where we cannot list all cases exhaustively. However, it is recommended you don't abuse the wildcard pattern as it will prevent the compiler from helping us when we forget a case in a matching expression.

This is very much similar to the `default` case in the `switch...case` statement in C#.

Tuples

Tuples are the simplest data type. A tuple is just an anonymous collection of values of arbitrary types. For example, the following is a tuple of `int` and `string`:

```
> let e = 1001, "John Smith";;
val e : int * string = 1001, "John Smith"
```

There are built-in functions, such as `fst` and `snd`, that return the first and the second components of a two-element tuple, respectively.

```
> let employeeId = fst e;;
val employeeId : int = 1001
> let employeeName = snd e;;
val employeeName : string = "John Smith"
```

The `fst` and `snd` functions are generic, so they can be applied to a pair of any `'a * 'b` type.

There are no similar functions for other tuples that are greater than two elements.

Value matching

As we saw earlier, a tuple creates a value out of two or more other values but, outside the `fst` and `snd` functions, we do not know yet how to access the tuple components. Now is when the real power of matching expressions comes into its own, as they are useful not only for matching a value with a pattern but also for *destructuring* it. Consider the following example for a tuple:

```
let compare_xy (xy: int*int) =
    match xy with
    | (0, _) -> "x is zero"
    | (_, 0) -> "y is zero"
    | _      -> "x and y are different than zero"
> compare_xy 0 10;;
val it: string = "x is zero"
```

Here, we have made the type of the `xy` argument explicit: an `int*int` tuple.

With tuples, we often just want to set the components apart. As here there is only one possible case, we can inline the matching expression, for example in a `let` binding or as a function argument:

```
> let employeeId, employeeName = e;;
val employeeId : int = 1001
val employeeName : string = John Smith
```

If there are some components that we are not interested in, we can use the following wildcard pattern to ignore them:

```
> let _, employeeName = e;;
val employeeName : string = John Smith
```

There are many data structures that we can use pattern matching with, such as lists or arrays. Patterns can also be nested; for example, a tuple pattern can appear within a list pattern. Later, we will see how we can match and destructure more complex types.

```
let tupleList = [(0,1); (1,0)]
match tupleList with
| [(0, _); (_, 0)] -> printfn "Match found"
| _                -> printfn "Match not found"
```

As you can see in the preceding example, in F# commas are used only for tuples while semicolons separate elements in a collection. This can be a bit confusing when starting to learn the language.

Records

As record is a special form of class definition for the ML languages. A record type is like a tuple where the elements are named. For example, let's declare an `Employee` record type, which is as follows:

```
type Employee =
    {
        firstName    : string
        lastName     : string
        gender       : string
        phoneNumber  : string
        salary       : float
    }
```

Unlike tuples, records cannot be built on the fly and must be declared in advance. The syntax to instantiate a record value is similar to the type definition, but the fields are defined as `label = expr`. An employee example is shown as follows:

```
let emp =
    {
        firstName    = "John"
        lastName     = "Smith"
        gender       = "M"
        phoneNumber  = "0115671234"
        salary       = 10.0
    }
```

The F# compiler automatically infers the `Employee` type by comparing the labels with the types available in the scope.

We can then access the fields as follows:

```
> emp.firstName;;
val it : string = "John"
```

Updating records

The following are the two ways to update records:

- Functional update
- Mutable fields

Functional update

The syntax for a functional update uses the `with` keyword in a record definition. It creates a copy of a record with new values for the specified fields, as follows:

```
> let dave = { emp with firstName = "Dave"; salary = 12.0 };;
val dave : Employee = {firstName = "Dave";
                       lastName = "Smith";
                       gender = "M";
                       phoneNumber = "0115671234";
                       salary = 12.0;}
```

Mutable fields

Record fields can also be modified by assignment, but it is mandatory to mark the field type as `mutable`. For example, if we want to modify the following `salary` field, we will declare it as `mutable`:

```
type Employee =
    {
        firstName   : string
        lastName    : string
        gender      : string
        phoneNumber : string
        mutable salary    : float
    }
```

Reinitializing the same employee value here will allow us to modify the following `salary` field without creating copies:

```
> emp.salary <- 14.0;;
```

Field label declarations

It is important to understand field label declarations. As the F# type inference automatically figures out the record based on the field definitions, if we have declared two different records with the same field names, then the F# will take the latest reference of the type with the field names. Let's consider the following example:

```
> type Person1 = { name: string; age: int };;
type Person1 =
  {name: string;
   age: int;}
> let p1 = { name = "John Smith"; age = 10 };;
val p1 : Person1 = {name = "John Smith";
                         age = 10;}
> type Person2 = { name: string; age: int };;
type Person2 =
  {name: string;
   age: int;}
> let p2 = { name = "John Smith"; age = 10 };;
val p2 : Person2 = {name = "John Smith";
                         age = 10;}
```

As we have declared two record types with the same labels, the F# compiler will pick the one that was declared last. To remove the ambiguity, we can prefix one of the labels with the name of the following type:

```
> let p3 = { Person1.name = "John Smith"; age = 10 };;
   val p3 : Person1 = {name = "John Smith";
                            age = 10;}
```

Value matching

F# records also allow pattern matching using the following `match` condition:

```
type Point = {
        x: int
        y: int
    }

let isEmptyPoint p =
    match p with
    | { x = 0; y = 0 }  -> true
    | _                 -> false
> isEmptyPoint { x = 0; y = 0 };;
val it : bool = true
> isEmptyPoint { x = 10; y = 10 };;
```

```
val it : bool = false
```

It is possible to match only specific fields in the record. In the following sample, note that the first x is the pattern matching the name of the label, while the second x' is where we project the field content:

```
let { x = x' } = p
```

Common Language Infrastructure mutable records

F# allows a record type to be marked with the [<CLIMutable>] attribute. This is useful when we require an empty constructor in F# records for use-cases where we want to serialize the data or interface with a C# library.

Union cases

Unions are also called tagged unions or algebraic data types. They are an important part of the F# type system. If tuples and records represent the intersection of several types, unions represent the sum of several types, meaning that instances of the union type can take the shape of only one of the types in the group at a time. The following is the syntax for a union type:

```
type typename =
| Identifier1 of type1
| Identifier2 of type2
|...
|...
| IdentifierN of typeN
```

Each case has an identifier, tag, or optionally a type argument. Cases should be capitalized. Let's take a very simple example of defining a AlphaNumeric type, which is as follows:

```
type AlphaNumeric =
    | Alphabet of string
    | Numeric   of int
```

Values in a union are declared as follows:

```
let CharA = Alphabet "A"
// val CharA : AlphaNumeric = Alphabet "A"
let Number = Numeric 1
// val Number : AlphaNumeric = Numeric 1
```

Patterns also use the identifier name. For example, we can define a pattern-matching function that checks for alphabets, as follows:

```
let isAlphabet x =
    match x with
    | Alphabet (_) -> true
    | _            -> false
// val isAlphabet : x:AlphaNumeric -> bool
```

Patterns can also be nested, allowing for much more expressivity while matching union types:

```
type Number =
    | Zero
    | Integer   of int
    | Real      of float


let add t1 t2 =
    match t1, t2 with
    | Zero, n | n, Zero -> n
    | Integer i1, Integer i2 -> Integer(i1 + i2)
    | Integer i, Real r -> Real (r + (float i))
    | Real r, Integer i -> Real (r + (float i))
    | Real r1, Real r2 -> Real (r1 + r2)
val add : t1:Number -> t2:Number -> Number

> add (Integer 10) (Real 20.);;
val it : Number = Real 30.0
```

As we can see, union types provide a very nice abstraction and declarative way to define the type and use pattern matching. We will see more advanced data structures in the next chapter that use union types to build immutable data structures. Some of the most important, built-in F# union types are `Option` and `list` (we will explore them in more detail in future chapters).

In Chapter 3, *Data Structures in F#*, we will look into building data structures easily with union cases.

Options in F#

The F# `Option` type is defined as a union case with two options: `Some` and `None`. The type definition of an F# `Option` type is as follows:

```
type Option<'a> =
    | Some of 'a
    | None
```

As you can see, `Option` is a generic type. F# generics work as in other .NET languages and represent a placeholder that can be filled with another type, making it possible to write polymorphic code that works with different types while keeping most of the benefits of strongly typing. The main difference with generics in C#, for example, is that the F# generic placeholder must be prefixed with an apostrophe. The `Option` type can be used in the same way as a union type, which is as follows:

```
let intVal = Some 1
let notInt = None

let isSome x =
    match x with
    | Some(_) -> true
    | None    -> false
```

In F#, `Option` types are used instead of nullable objects. Let's consider the following code as an example:

```
let x : string = null
let len = x.Length

let x2 = Option<string>.None
let len2 = x2.Length
```

The first two lines will compile without a problem but will throw a `NullReferenceException` at runtime. However the last two will throw a compile-time error because F# forces users to unwrap `Option` types to use them. We can use the following pattern matching for that:

```
let len2 =
    match x2 with
    | Some(t) -> t.Length
    | _       -> 0
```

Note that, when pattern matching, we will need to take into consideration both cases: when the option contains a value and when the option does not contain a value. This helps us write null-free code and thus, with few bugs. Additionally, the `Option` module provides several higher-order functions that can be used to overcome the issues with nullable types.

`val bind : ('T -> 'U option)   -> 'T option -> 'U option`	**This invokes a function on an optional value that itself yields an option**
`val get : 'T option -> 'T`	This gets the value associated to the `option`
`val isNone : 'T option ->   bool`	This returns `true` if the option is `None`
`val isSome : 'T option ->   bool`	This returns `true` if the option is `Some`
`val map : ('T -> 'V) -> 'T   option -> 'V option`	This transforms an option value by applying the `map` function
`val iter : ('T -> unit) ->   'T option -> unit`	This executes a function for an option value

Structural equality and comparison

F# defines a list of equality and comparison operators, which is as follows:

```
(=)    : 'T -> 'T -> bool when 'T : equality
(<>)   : 'T -> 'T -> bool when 'T : equality
hash   : 'T -> int when 'T : equality
(<)    : 'T -> 'T -> bool when 'T : comparison
(<=)   : 'T -> 'T -> bool when 'T : comparison
(>)    : 'T -> 'T -> bool when 'T : comparison
(>=)   : 'T -> 'T -> bool when 'T : comparison
compare : 'T -> 'T -> int when 'T : comparison
min     : 'T -> 'T -> 'T when 'T : comparison
max     : 'T -> 'T -> 'T when 'T : comparison
```

These are generic types and thus we can use them in any .NET type. The signatures also contain constraints, which exclude some types as candidates for the `'T` placeholder (in this case, the type must implement equality and comparison methods respectively). Some important F# generic types such as `Set<'T>` and `Map<'Key, 'Value>` also have structural `equality` and `comparison` constraints.

In the F# core library, equality and comparison operators are conditional on the structure of types. For example, we can only use the preceding equality and comparison operators on a tuple if the constituent parts of the tuple also support equality and comparison. We can consider four different types of equality, which are as follows:

- For some types, equality is structural, meaning that two values will be deemed identical if they have the same content, for example, records, tuples, lists, and so on
- For some types, equality is referenced, meaning that two values will be considered identical only if they share the same reference (they point to the same direction in memory), for example, classes
- For some types, equality is customized, for example, types implementing a custom `Equals` method

For some types, no equality or comparison are applicable.

For most cases, we can assume that F# core types, such as tuples, lists, records, unions, and so on (plus arrays and structs), implement structural equality and comparison, while interfaces and .NET classes have reference equality. However, as mentioned earlier, depending on the structure of the type, this may not hold true. We can enforce structural equality or comparison by using the `StructuralEquality` or `StructuralComparison` attributes. This code runs without problems:

```
[<StructuralEquality;StructuralComparison>]
type EmployeeObject = Age of int
```

However, the preceding example gives an error at compile time. The type can't logically support automatic structural comparison because one of the element types does not support structural equality or comparison:

```
type Employee() = class end

[<StructuralEquality;StructuralComparison>]
type EmployeeRelationship = EmployeeRelation of int * string *  string
* Employee
```

Here, `Employee` is a normal F# class that doesn't implement the `equality` and `comparison` constraints.

F# function types don't support equality and comparison.

We can also declare that a structural type should use the `ReferenceEquality` attribute, which is as follows:

```
[<ReferenceEquality>]
type EmployeeManager = EmployeeManager of Employee * (int -> int)
```

The following table shows the attributes that we can use to modify the default behavior of types for equality and comparison:

`StructuralEquality,` `StructuralComparison`	**This indicates a structural type that must support equality and/or comparison**
`ReferenceEquality`	This indicates a structural type that supports only reference equality
`NoComparison, NoEquality`	This indicates a type that doesn't support equality or comparison at all
`CustomEquality, CustomComparison`	This indicates a structural type that supports custom equality and/or comparison

Custom equality and comparison

Sometimes, we may need to define custom equality and comparison techniques. Let's extend our `Employee` record type to define a custom `equality` constraint:

```
[<CustomEquality; CustomComparison>]
type EmployeeType =
    { EmployeeId: int;
      Name: string }

    override this.Equals(y) =
        match y with
        | :? EmployeeType as other -> (this.EmployeeId =
            other.EmployeeId)
        | _ -> false

    override x.GetHashCode() = hash x.EmployeeId

    interface System.IComparable with
      member x.CompareTo y = compare x (y :?> EmployeeType)
```

Reference cells and side-effects

Most of the types that we have seen so far are immutable in nature. In this section, we will look at different ways to do some imperative programming with reference cells and mutable values. Reference cells in F# can be viewed as boxes holding a value that can be replaced by some other value. The basic operations on reference cells are as follows:

```
val ref : 'a -> 'a ref
val (:=) : 'a ref -> 'a -> unit
val (!) : 'a ref -> 'a
```

Reference cells are created with the `ref` e expression, which takes an initial value of e. The `:=` expression is used to update the content of a reference cell, and the `!` operator returns the current value of the cell.

A side-effect is a notion in which the state of a variable or an object is modified from its current state. A function with side effects doesn't resemble a mathematical function because *f(0)* may not always be the same as *f(0)*.

Reasoning about imperative programs can be more difficult than it is for pure functional programs because they modify the state of the program. As pure functions are guaranteed to produce the same output given the same input and without side-effects, we can just replace a function call in our code with its output. Pure functional programs are referentially transparent and have many benefits. This is known as referential transparency. Also, in functional programming, data structures are persistent as data once created is not changed or destroyed.

However, side effects can sometimes be useful to reduce the code size and provide better memory management when resources are scarce. F# is not a pure functional language, as it allows us to produce side effects if necessary. For example, we can easily implement a useful data structure that keeps mutable state, such as a `Queue`, as follows:

```
type Queue<'T> = | Q of 'T array ref

let create<'t>() =
    Queue<'t>.Q( ref Array.empty )

let push queue t =
    match queue with
    | Q(x) ->
        let r = !x
        x := Array.append r [|t|]
        Q( x )

let pop queue =
```

```
        match queue with
        | Q(x) ->
            let r = !x
            let a = Seq.head r
            x := (Seq.skip 1 r) |> Seq.toArray
            a
```

The following is an example of the usage of Queue:

```
> let tq = create<int>();;
val tq : Queue<int> = Q {contents = [||];}

> push tq 10;;
val it : Queue<int> = Q {contents = [|10|];}

> push tq 20;;
val it : Queue<int> = Q {contents = [|10; 20|];}

> let f = pop tq;;
val f : int = 10

> tq;;
val it : Queue<int> = Q {contents = [|20|];}
```

Active patterns

Active patterns are special types of patterns where the result of the pattern match is dependent on a function of the input. We will use banana clips, as in (|Even|Odd|), to define a function for use in pattern matching. Let's consider the following example:

```
let (|Even|Odd|) input = if input % 2 = 0 then Even else Odd
    let testNumber = function
        | Even -> sprintf "%d is even" input
        | Odd -> sprintf "%d is odd" input
```

Partial active patterns

We can use a wildcard character to define a partial active pattern; they have a return value of the Option type. To define a partial active pattern, you will use a wildcard character (_) at the end of the list of patterns inside the banana clips, as follows:

```
let (|Integer|_|) (str: string) =
    match System.Int32.TryParse str with
    | true, x -> Some x
    | false, _ -> None
```

```
let (|Float|_|) (str: string) =
    match System.Double.TryParse str with
    | true, x -> Some x
    | false, _ -> None

let parseNumeric = function
    | Integer i -> sprintf "%d : Integer" i
    | Float f -> sprintf "%f : Floating point" f
    | _ -> sprintf "%s : Not matched." str
```

Let's test the following piece of code in **F# Interactive** window:

```
> parseNumeric "1.1"
1.100000 : Floating point
> parseNumeric "0"
0 : Integer
```

Additionally, active patterns can take the following parameters:

```
open System.Text.RegularExpressions
let (|FirstRegexGroup|_|) pattern input =
    let m = Regex.Match(input,pattern)
    if (m.Success) then Some m.Groups.[1].Value else None
let testRegex str =
    match str with
    | FirstRegexGroup "http://(.*?)/(.*)" host ->
            printfn "The value is a url and the host is %s"
            host
    | _ -> printfn "no matching patterns"
```

Summary

In this chapter, we went through some of the functional aspects of F#, such as immutable data structures, structural equality, and pattern matching. We also explored as how we can write a more imperative style when needed, such as keeping internal state with reference cells or mutable data structures. In the next chapter, you will learn more about other data structures that are very important in F#: collections.

3

Data Structures in F#

We have seen different ways to perform functional programming with F#. In this chapter, we will cover the following data structures and writing custom data structures in a more concise and readable way:

- F# `Collections`
- `Seq`, `Array`, `List`, `Map`, `Set`
- `yield` keyword
- Advanced data structures
- Stacks
- Queues
- Binary search trees
- Red-black tree

This chapter just helps you understand how to use the available data structures in F# and write some basic custom data structures. As a developer, it will help you think more in functional aspects inclined towards type safety, immutability, and other areas that you learned in the previous chapters.

F# Collections

F# core library has a set of collections and wrapper functional style modules that are useful. In this chapter, we will go through the basic list of collection modules with examples and understand their inner workings.

The following is a basic list of collection modules:

- `Seq`: This performs basic operations on any collection implementing `IEnumerable<'T>`
- `Array`: This performs basic operations on `Array` collections
- `List`: This performs basic operations on `List` collections
- `Map`: This performs functional style operators for the `Map` type
- `Set`: This performs functional style operators for the `Set` type

Sequence

Sequence is a logical series of elements of the same type. Sequences are lazy in nature and always iterate a single element at any given time, so it has better performance over large collections when compared to arrays or lists. Sequences are basically the .NET `IEnumerable<'T>` collections that have an alias `seq<'T>` type in F#. The `Seq` module provides several helper functions to work with the sequence collections.

Sequence expressions

Sequence expressions are a construct in F # to generate sequences. A simple example can be `seq { 1 .. 5 }`, which generates a sequence of integers from one to five. We can use the `yield` keyword inside sequence expressions to return the following values:

```
let intSeqs =
    seq {
        for i = 0 to 10 do
            yield i * 2
    }
```

We can also add the following `if` conditions inside sequence expressions, modifying the same example:

```
let intSeqs2 =
    seq {
        for i = 0 to 10 do
            if i % 2 = 0 then
                yield i * 2
    }
```

Sequence expressions can also be used with arrays or lists. This will be covered in more detail in the further topics.

Working with Seq functions

All the collection data types in .NET implement the `IEnumerable<'T>` interface and hence all the enumerable collections can be accepted by the `Seq` module. The `Seq` module also supports other operations, such as grouping or counting, using key-generating functions.

Creating sequences

We can create sequences using the sequence expressions as defined earlier, and also with functions from the `Seq` module. We will see some samples and run them in F# interactive. First, we will code a little helper to print a whole sequence, as follows:

```
> let printSeq t = Seq.iter (printfn "%A") t;;
```

The `Seq.iter` function applies a given function to each of the sequence's elements. Let's take a look at some functions for creating a sequence:

- `Seq.init: count:int -> initializer:(int -> 'T) -> seq<'T>`: This creates a sequence and gives a length and function initializer to generate the elements:

  ```
  > let seqMultiplesOfFive = Seq.init 5 (fun i -> i * 5);;
  > printSeq seqMultiplesOfFive;;
  0 5 10 15 20
  ```

- `Seq.cast: source:System.Collections.IEnumerable -> seq<'T>`: This type casts a weak-typed collection, such as those generated from the `System.Collections` namespace to a strongly-typed `seq<'T>` type:

  ```
  >arrayList = new System.Collections.ArrayList();;
  > for i in 1 .. 10 do arrayList.Add(i) |> ignore;;
  > let seqInt : seq<int> = Seq.cast arrayList;;
  > printSeq seqInt;;
  1 2 3 4 5 6 7 8 9 10
  ```

- `Seq.unfold: generator:('State -> ('T * 'State) option) -> state:'State -> seq<'T>`: This generates a sequence based on an initial state. For the first iteration, the value passed is the initial state, and the generator function returns a tuple option of the next element in the sequence and the next state value. Returning `None` finishes the sequence.

  ```
  > let values = Seq.unfold (fun state -> if state > 10 then None
  else Some (state, 2 + state)) 0;;
  ```

```
> printSeq values::
0 2 4 6 8 10
```

Searching and finding elements

The Seq module provides some functions to search, filter, and find elements from an existing sequence. The following are some of the mostly used functions:

- Seq.filter: predicate:('T -> bool) -> source:seq<'T> -> seq<'T>: This applies a predicate function to a sequence and returns a new sequence with only the values that fulfil the predicate:

  ```
  > let values = Seq.init 10 (fun i -> i * 5);;
  > let filteredValues = Seq.filter (fun x -> x % 2 = 0) values;;
  > printSeq filteredValues;;
  0 10 20 30 40
  ```

- Seq.find: predicate:('T -> bool) -> source:seq<'T> -> 'T: This returns the first element fulfilling the given predicate in a sequence. If the element is not found, then it throws an exception, as follows:

  ```
  seq { 1 .. 5 } |> Seq.find (fun i -> i > 3);;
  val it : int = 4
  ```

- Seq.tryFind: predicate:('T -> bool) -> source:seq<'T> -> 'T option: This is just like Seq.find, but it returns Option. It returns None if no value is not found:

  ```
  seq { 1 .. 5 } |> Seq.find (fun i -> i > 3);;
  var it: int option = None
  ```

- Seq.findIndex: predicate:('T -> bool) -> source:seq<'T> -> int: This finds the index of the element fulfilling the given predicate in the sequence, and if it is not found, then it throws an exception, as follows:

  ```
  seq { 1 .. 5 } |> Seq.findIndex (fun i -> i > 3);;
  val it : int = 4
  ```

- `Seq.tryFindIndex: predicate:('T -> bool) -> source:seq<'T> -> int option`: Like `Seq.findIndex`, it returns `Option`. It returns `None` if no value is found:

```
seq { 1 .. 5 } |> Seq.findIndex (fun i -> i > 6);;
var it: int option = None
```

- `Seq.truncate: count:int -> source:seq<'T> -> seq<'T>`: This truncates an existing sequence by returning, at most, the first N elements. The following example returns the first five elements of a sequence which contains ten elements:

```
> let values = Seq.init 10 (fun i -> i * 5);;
> let truncedValues = Seq.truncate 5 values;;
> printSeq truncedValues;;
0 5 10 15 20
```

- `Seq.skip: count:int -> source:seq<'T> -> seq<'T>`: This skips the first N values of a sequence.
- `Seq.take: count:int -> source:seq<'T> -> seq<'T>`: This takes only the first N values of a sequence, as follows:

```
> let values = Seq.init 100 (fun i -> i * 5);;
> let skippedValues =
            values
            |> Seq.skip 5
            |> Seq.take 10;;
> printSeq skippedValues;;
25 30 35 40 45 50 55 60 65 70
```

- `Seq.skipWhile, Seq.takeWhile`: Both these functions perform the same functionality as skip and take, but with a predicate condition, as follows:

```
> let values = Seq.init 100 (fun i -> i * 5);;
> let skippedValues =
            values
            |> Seq.skipWhile(fun el -> el < 25)
            |> Seq.takeWhile(fun el -> el < 75);;
> printSeq skippedValues;;
25 30 35 40 45 50 55 60 65 70
```

Sequence generators

Generator functions transform a sequence into another sequence of elements. Let's take a look at a few of the functions, which are as follows:

- `Seq.map: mapping:('T -> 'U) -> source:seq<'T> -> seq<'U>`: This creates a new sequence by transforming each element of the input sequence with the given function, as follows:

```
> seq { 1 .. 5 } |> Seq.map (fun i -> 'A' + char i) |>
printSeq;;
'B' 'C' 'D' 'E' 'F'
```

- `Seq.choose: chooser:('T -> 'U option) -> source:seq<'T> -> seq<'U>`: This is a combination of `Seq.map` and `Seq.filter` functions, as the given function acts at the same time as a mapper and a predicate (when `None` is returned the element gets discarded):

```
> seq { 1 .. 10 }
|> Seq.choose (fun i -> if i % 2 = 0 then Some('A' + char i)
else None)
|> printSeq;;
'C' 'E' 'G' 'I' 'K'
```

- `Seq.pairwise: source:seq<'T> -> seq<'T * 'T>`: This creates a new sequence in which successive elements of the input are grouped as tuples:

```
> let values = Seq.init 10 (fun i -> i * 5);;
> let pairWise = Seq.pairwise values;;
> printSeq pairWise;;
(0, 5) (5, 10) (10, 15) (15, 20) (20, 25) (25, 30) (30, 35)
(35,40) (40, 45)
```

- `Seq.windowed: windowSize:int -> source:seq<'T> -> seq<'T []>`: This is similar to pairwise, except it generates a sequence of arrays of *N* adjacent elements:

```
> let values = Seq.init 10 (fun i -> i * 5);;
> let windows = Seq.windowed 3 values;;
> printSeq windows;;
[|0; 5; 10|] [|5; 10; 15|] [|10; 15; 20|] [|15; 20; 25|] [|20;
25; 30|] [|25; 30; 35|] [|30; 35; 40|] [|35; 40; 45|]
```

Sequence computation operations

The `Seq` module also provides functions such as `fold`, `reduce`, `sort`, `sortBy`, `compareWith`, `groupBy`, `countBy`, `average`, `sum`, `averageBy`, and `sumBy`, which are similar to LINQ operations on collections:

- `Seq.fold: folder:('State -> 'T -> 'State) -> initialState:'State -> source:seq<'T> -> 'State`: This produces a single value by combining all the elements of the sequence using the given function where the inputs are the current state and element:

```
>    seq { 1..5 } |> Seq.fold (fun state i -> state + i) 5;;
val it : int = 20
```

- `Seq.reduce: reduction:('T -> 'T -> 'T) -> source:seq<'T> -> 'T`: This is similar to `Seq.fold`, but without the initial state. The first element in the sequences becomes the initial state:

```
>    seq { 1..5 } |> Seq.reduce (fun state i -> state + i);;
val it : int = 15
```

- `Seq.sort: source:seq<'T> -> seq<'T> (requires comparison)`: This sorts a sequence of elements that are comparable by default, such as numeric values or strings. In this example, we will use a stepped range (*start .. step .. range*) to generate a downward sequence that will be sorted with `Seq.sort`:

```
> seq { 5..-1..1 } |> Seq.sort |> printSeq;;
1 2 3 4 5
```

- `Seq.sortBy: projection:('T -> 'Key) -> source:seq<'T> -> seq<'T> (requires comparison)`: This sorts a sequence of elements by first projecting each element to do the comparison. In this example, again, we will use an increasing sequence, but it will be sorted in a decreasing order because the project is taking the negative value of each item before comparison:

```
> seq { 1..5 } |> Seq.sortBy (fun i -> -i) |> printSeq;;
5 4 3 2 1
```

- Seq.compareWith: comparer:('T -> 'T -> int) -> source1:seq<'T> -> source2:seq<'T> -> int: This compares two sequences using the given function. If the function returns a negative value, it means the first input is smaller than the second and vice versa if it is a positive value (0 means both inputs are identical):

```
> let compareSeq t1 t2 =
      Seq.compareWith(fun e1 e2 ->
          if e1 > e2 then 1
          else if e1 < e2 then -1
          else 0
      ) t1 t2;;
> let v1 = Seq.init 10 (fun i -> i * 5);;
> let v2 = Seq.init 10 (fun i -> i * 3);;
> let r = compareSeq v1 v2;;
val r : int = 1
```

- Seq.groupBy: projection:('T -> 'Key) -> source:seq<'T> -> seq<'Key * seq<'T>> (requires equality): This groups a sequence based on the key comparer function. The following example shows a sequence of integers grouped by testing if they are even or odd:

```
> let v = seq { 1.. 20 };;
> let grouped = Seq.groupBy(fun i -> if i % 2 = 0 then 0 else 1)
v;;
> printSeq grouped;;
(1, seq [1; 3; 5; 7; ...]) (0, seq [2; 4; 6; 8; ...])
```

- Seq.countBy: projection:('T -> 'Key) -> source:seq<'T> -> seq<'Key * int> (requires equality): This projects each element and counts the number of times the same projection happens in the sequence:

```
> seq { 1..20 } |> Seq.countBy(fun i -> if i % 2 = 0 then 0 else
1);;
seq [(1, 10); (0, 10)]
```

Arrays

Arrays are fixed sized vectors as they can be commonly found in other languages, such as C# or Java. Arrays are usually very efficient, but you must be aware of two facts—unlike sequences, they are not immutable and they are not lazy, so they need enough memory space to fit all its elements.

We can create an array by entering elements of the same type in a consecutive way surrounded by the `[| |]` symbols and separated by semicolons; this is important because other languages often use commas for that, and in F#, commas are only for tuples:

```
> let intArray = [| 1;2;3 |];;
```

We can also define the array with line breaks instead of semi-colons:

```
> let intArray2 =
        [|
              1
              2
              3
        |];;
```

Fields in arrays can be accessed by an `.[i]` construct. Array indexes start from 0, and the .NET common language runtime ensures that the indexes are within the bounds of an array or it will throw an exception:

```
> intArray.[0];;
val it : int = 1
```

Fields are updated with the following `a.[i] <- value` assignment construct:

```
> intArray.[1] <- 10;;
> intArray.[1];;
val it : int = 10
```

F# also provides slice notation in which we can access a set of the following values from the array:

```
> intArray.[0..2];;
val it : int [] = [|1; 2; 3|]
```

We can also create arrays using comprehensions, as follows:

```
> let intArraySliced = [| 0..10 |]
val intArraySliced : int [] = [|0; 1; 2; 3; 4; 5; 6; 7; 8; 9; 10|]
```

Working with Array functions

The `Array` module defines a set of additional functions on arrays. To create or initialize an array in which all elements can be 0, we can write a code snippet as follows:

```
> let arrayOfZeros : int[] = Array.zeroCreate 10;;
val arrayOfZeros : int [] = [|0; 0; 0; 0; 0; 0; 0; 0; 0; 0|]
```

The following is a list of some of the functions from the `Array` module:

- `Array.create`: This creates an array of a specified size and sets all the elements to the provided value, as follows:

```
> let intArray3 = Array.create 10 3;;
val intArray3 : int [] = [|3; 3; 3; 3; 3; 3; 3; 3; 3; 3|]
```

- `Array.init`: This creates an array and given a length and a function initializer to generate the elements, as follows:

```
> let intArray4 = Array.init 10 (fun x -> x / 2)
val intArray4 : int [] = [|0; 0; 1; 1; 2; 2; 3; 3; 4; 4|]
```

- `Array.sub`: This generates a new array from a subrange of the array:

```
> let t1 = [| 0..10 |];;
val t1 : int [] = [|0; 1; 2; 3; 4; 5; 6; 7; 8; 9; 10|]
> let t2 = Array.sub t1 1 4;;
val t2 : int [] = [|1; 2; 3; 4|]
```

- `Array.append`: This creates a new array by appending two arrays:

```
> let a1 = [| 0..5 |];;
val a1 : int [] = [|0; 1; 2; 3; 4; 5|]
> let a2 = [| 6..10|];;
val a2 : int [] = [|6; 7; 8; 9; 10|]
> let a3 = Array.append a1 a2;;
val a3 : int [] = [|0; 1; 2; 3; 4; 5; 6; 7; 8; 9; 10|]
```

- `Array.concat`: This takes a sequence of arrays and combines them into a single array:

```
> let cc1 = Array.init 2 (fun x -> [| 0..x |]);;
val cc1 : int [] [] = [|[|0|]; [|0; 1|]|]
> let cc2 = Array.concat cc1;;
val cc2 : int [] = [|0; 0; 1|]
```

- `Array.collect`: This applies a function that returns a new array for each element of another array and concatenates all results at the end. The following example shows an array generator based on another `cl1` array, which is used as an initializer:

```
> let cl1 = [| 1; 10|];;
val cl1 : int [] = [|1; 10|]
> let cl2 = Array.collect (fun e -> [| 0..e |]) cl1;;
```

```
val cl2 : int [] = [|0; 1; 0; 1; 2; 3; 4; 5; 6; 7; 8; 9; 10|]
```

- `Array.filter`: This takes a predicate and returns a new array with only the elements that fulfill the predicate:

```
> let f1 = Array.init 10 (fun x -> x * 15);;
val f1 : int [] = [|0; 15; 30; 45; 60; 75; 90; 105; 120; 135|]
> let f2 = Array.filter(fun x -> x % 2 = 0) f1;;
val f2 : int [] = [|0; 30; 60; 90; 120|]
```

- `Array.choose`: This a combination of `Array.map` and `Array.filter`. It selects and transforms elements based on a filter criteria and creates a new array, which is as follows:

```
> let c1 = [| 0..10 |];;
val c1 : int [] = [|0; 1; 2; 3; 4; 5; 6; 7; 8; 9; 10|]
> let c2 = Array.choose (fun el -> if el % 2 = 0 then Some(el)
else None) c1;;
val c2 : int [] = [|0; 2; 4; 6; 8; 10|]
```

- `Array.rev`: This reverses the array, as follows:

```
> let r1 = [| 1..10 |];;
val r1 : int [] = [|1; 2; 3; 4; 5; 6; 7; 8; 9; 10|]
> let r2 = Array.rev r1;;
val r2 : int [] = [|10; 9; 8; 7; 6; 5; 4; 3; 2; 1|]
```

We can also combine array functions using the following |> pipeline operator, which looks much more concise:

```
> [| 1..10 |]
|> Array.choose (fun el -> if el % 2 = 0 then Some(el) else None)
|> Array.collect (fun e -> [| 0..e |])
|> Array.rev
|> printfn "%A";;
[|10; 9; 8; 7; 6; 5; 4; 3; 2; 1; 0; 8; 7; 6; 5; 4; 3; 2; 1; 0; 6; 5; 4; 3;
2; 1;
  0; 4; 3; 2; 1; 0; 2; 1; 0|]
```

Arrays can be converted to lists or sequences and vice versa with functions such as `Array.ofList`, `Array.ofSeq`, `Array.toList`, and `Array.toSeq`.

Arrays and tuples

The `Array.zip` and `Array.unzip` functions convert arrays of tuple pairs to tuples of arrays and vice versa. The `Array.zip3` and `Array.unzip3` functions work with tuples of three elements. The following example shows how to use `Array.zip` to multiply two sets of arrays:

```
> Array.zip  [| 1..10 |] [| 11..20 |];;
val it : (int * int) [] = [|(1, 11); (2, 12); (3, 13); (4, 14); (5, 15);
(6, 16); (7, 17); (8, 18); (9, 19); (10, 20)|]
```

Array comprehensions

Array comprehensions can be used as array generators as well. As we have already seen, we will use the `yield` keyword to return an item from the expression. The following is a simple example that generates an array out of multiples of 2 and 3:

```
> [| for i = 0 to 10 do
        yield i * 2
        yield i * 3
|];;
val it : int [] =
 [|0; 0; 2; 3; 4; 6; 6; 9; 8; 12; 10; 15; 12; 18; 14; 21; 16; 24; 18; 27;
20; 30|]
```

Array.Parallel module

This module contains some of the functions of the `Array` module, but executes operations in parallel, which has better performance when we are manipulating large arrays on a multicore machine:

- `Init`: This initializes an array from the given dimension and functor.
- `Iter`: This iterates the array and applies the function to each element.
- `Iteri`: This is like `iter`, but it also passes the index of each element to the function.
- `map`: This builds a new array by applying a functor to each element in the array.
- `mapi`: This is like `map`, but it also passes the index of each element to the mapping function.
- `choose`: This is like `map`, but the mapping function returns an option. When the function returns `None`, the element is discarded.

- `collect`: This applies the given function and concatenate all the results for each element of the array.
- `partition`: This splits the array into two collections, one for containing the `true` predicate and the other one for the `false` predicate.

Lists

Lists are another type of collections often used in F#. They are not to be confused with .NET `System.Collections.Generic.List` that have the `ResizeArray` alias in F# as the behavior is very different. As arrays, lists are not lazy and take the whole memory space necessary to fit all the elements. The biggest difference is that lists are immutable, so they work better with the functional programming style. As mutation is not allowed, every time we need to make a modification to the list, we will need to make a new copy. To avoid the performance penalty of making too many copies of the collection, lists work as linked collections. Meaning, each element contains a link to the next, and so on until the end of the collection. This makes it more efficient to make a new copy of the list by appending one or more elements to the list because (thanks to the immutable nature of lists) the new list can just link to the old one and share the memory space.

Lists constructors have a special syntax in F#, there are two of them:

- `[]`: This denotes empty list
- `h :: t`: This is called a cons operation; it creates a cons cell where the first element is the head and the rest is a list of the same type

We can also declare a list by surrounding the elements with brackets `[]`, as follows:

```
> let intList = [1; 2; 3;];;
val intList : int list = [1; 2; 3]
> intList.Head;;
val it : int = 1
> intList.Tail;;
val it : int list = [2; 3]
```

Lists can be deconstructed in pattern matching. The following example shows a sum function for a list of ints:

```
> let rec sumOfList l =
    match l with
    | [] -> 0
    | h :: t -> h + (sumOfList t);;
> intList |> sumOfList;;
val it : int = 6
```

Arrays can also be deconstructed with pattern matching, but this is less common.

Lists can also be combined with tuples to represent a set of values. Deconstructing this in pattern matching is easy as well:

```
> let rec skipUntil (key: 'a) (x: ('a*'b) list) =
    match x with
    | (k, v) :: t ->
        if k = key then t
        else skipUntil key t
    | [] -> raise(new System.InvalidOperationException());;
> let data = [ (1,2); (2,3); (3,4) ];;
val data : (int * int) list = [(1, 2); (2, 3); (3, 4)]
> skipUntil 2 data;;
val it : (int * int) list = [(3, 4)]
```

The preceding example does a search on tuple elements with two items in it. The pattern matching `(k, v) :: t` should be read from outside-in. The pattern matching compares the first element `k` to the key value and returns the rest of the tail elements from the actual list if `k` is equal to the key. If the search doesn't find the key, then we will raise an exception.

Tail recursion

It is very common to use deep recursion when working with lists, so it is important to apply the tail recursion optimization to prevent stack overflows. As discussed in Chapter 1, *Getting Started with F#*, about tail recursion, it requires an accumulator value to be passed to the recursive function. Let's write a tail recursive map function, which is as follows:

```
let rec rev accum = function
    h :: t  -> rev (h :: accum) t
    | []    -> accum
let rec rev_map f accum = function
    h :: t  -> rev_map f (f h :: accum) t
    | []    -> accum

let map f l = rev [] (rev_map f [] l)
```

The `rev` function does a reverse on the list of objects, and `rev_map` maps a function to each item in the list and returns the processed listed in a reverse order. The `map` function does a reverse twice, one while applying the given function to each of the list's elements, and one to return the order of the elements to the original order so we get the output as given in the following sequence. This approach is much faster than the linear way of the `map` function:

```
> map (fun x -> x+1) [1;2;3];;
val it : int list = [2; 3; 4]
```

List and tuples

Lists with tuples can be manipulated by `zip` functions. The `List.zip`, `List.zip3`, `List.unzip`, and `List.unzip3` functions are useful to combine two lists or separate tuple lists into separate lists. The following code shows the usage of `List.zip`:

```
> let t1 = [1; 2; 3;];;
> let t2 = [4; 5; 6;];;
> let x = List.zip t1 t2;;
> printfn "%A" x;;
[(1, 4); (2, 5); (3, 6)]
```

The `List.unzip` function separates the tuples into individual lists; let's consider the following piece of code as an example:

```
> let lists = List.unzip [(1,2); (3,4)];;
> printfn "%A" lists;;
([1; 3], [2; 4])
```

Likewise, if we are working a three element tuple, then we will use the `List.zip3` and `List.unzip3` functions.

List comprehensions

Comprehensions can be used as list generators as well. As we have already seen, we will use the `yield` keyword to return an item from the expression. The following is a simple example that generates a list out of multiples of 2 and 3:

```
> [ for i = 0 to 10 do
      yield i * 2
      yield i * 3
  ]
val it : int list =
  [0; 0; 2; 3; 4; 6; 6; 9; 8; 12; 10; 15; 12; 18; 14; 21; 16; 24; 18; 27;
20; 30]
```

Sets

Sets are similar to lists, but they guarantee that every item in the collection is unique—when we try to add duplicated items, they are just ignored. The Set module also contains functions to perform union or intersect operations with other sets.

Sets can be created as follows:

```
> let simpleSet = Set.empty.Add(1).Add(20);;
val simpleSet : Set<int> = set [1; 20]
```

We can also initialize a Set module from List, Array, or Seq, as shown in the following piece of code:

```
> let setFromList = Set.ofList [1..20];;
val setFromList : Set<int> = set [1; 2; 3; 4; 5; 6; 7; 8; 9; ...]
```

The **Set** module provides a list of useful functionalities to manipulate sets, which are as follows:

- Set.compare
- Set.difference
- Set.filter
- Set.isSubset
- Set.intersect

The Set.compare and Set.difference functions are useful to compare and find differences between two sets; the Set.filter can be used to filter within a set; the Set.isSubset evaluates to true if all elements of a set are within the other set, and Set.intersect can be used to find the intersection between two sets:

```
> let s1 = Set.ofList [ 1 .. 10 ];;
> let s2 = Set.ofList [ 3..3..30 ];;
> let s3 = Set.intersect s1 s2;;
set [3; 6; 9]
```

Map

Maps is a special kind of set that associates keys with values. It is an immutable dictionary. A map is created in a similar way to a set, as shown in the following example:

```
> let simpleMap = Map.empty
                    .Add("1", "One")
                    .Add("2", "Two")
                    .Add("3", "Three");;
val simpleMap : Map<string,string> =
  map [("1", "One"); ("2", "Two"); ("3", "Three")]
```

A map is also created from a collection of tuples representing key value pairs, as shown in the following piece of code:

```
> [(1, "One"); (2; "Two"); (3, "Three")] |> Map;;
map [(1, "One"); (2, "Two"); (3, "Three")]
```

To access a value from the map, we will use the following indexer property as we do for arrays:

```
> simpleMap.["1"]
val it : string = "One"
```

Map can also be initialized from a `Seq`, `Array`, or a `List`, as follows:

```
> let mapFromList =
        [11 .. 20]
        |> List.zip [1 .. 10 ]
        |> Map.ofList
val mapFromList : Map<int,int> =
  map
    [(1, 11); (2, 12); (3, 13); (4, 14); (5, 15); (6, 16); (7, 17); (8,
18);
     (9, 19); ...]
```

F# sets and maps are implemented as immutable **automatic vehicle location** (**AVL**) trees, an efficient data structure that forms a self-balancing binary tree. AVL trees are well known for their efficiency, in which they can search, insert, and delete elements in the tree in $O(log\ n)$ time, where *n* is the number of elements in the tree.

Advanced data structures

You have learned to use data structures built-in in the `FSharp.Core` library; now you will learn how to define other advanced data structures on your own in F#.

Binary trees

Binary trees are often used to represent collections of data. For our purpose, a binary tree is an acyclic graph, in which each node has either zero or two children. The top-level node is called the **root**, and it has no parents, while all other nodes have exactly one parent. A simple way of representing a binary tree is as follows:

```
type 'a tree =
    | Leaf
    | Node of 'a * 'a tree * 'a tree
```

The use of tuples in the `Node` constructor definition is quite common. We will try to create some objects using this tree in the **F# Interactive**, as mentioned in the following piece of code:

```
> Node(1, Leaf, Leaf);;
val it : int tree = Node (1,Leaf,Leaf)
```

This creates an `int tree` with a top-level root node and empty leaves. As the type definition of `'a tree` is recursive, many of the functions defined on the tree can be recursive. For example, the following function defines one way to count the number of non-leaf nodes in the tree:

```
let cardinality (t: 'a tree) =
    let rec _cardinality = function
        | Leaf -> 0
        | Node(_, left, right) ->
            _cardinality left + _cardinality right + 1
    _cardinality t
> cardinality (Node(1, Node(2, Leaf, Leaf), Leaf));;
val it : int = 2
```

The empty set is just a leaf. To add an *X* element to a set, we will create a new node with a leaf as the left child and *X* as the right child:

```
let empty<'a> : 'a tree = Leaf

let rec insert h = function
    | Leaf -> Node(h, Leaf, Leaf)
    | Node(hd, l, r) -> Node(hd, l, insert h r)

let rec ofList = function
    | [] -> empty
    | h :: t -> insert h (ofList t)

> ofList [1;2;3;4];;
val it : int tree =
```

```
Node (4,Leaf,Node (3,Leaf,Node (2,Leaf,Node (1,Leaf,Leaf))))
```

The *isMemberOf* function is defined recursively to check if an x element is a member of the tree by checking the left and right nodes in the tree, as shown in the following block of code:

```
let rec isMemberOf x = function
  | Leaf -> false
  | Node(y, left, right) ->
      x = y || isMemberOf x left || isMemberOf x right

> let t = ofList [1;2;3;4];;
val t : int tree =
  Node (4,Leaf,Node (3,Leaf,Node (2,Leaf,Node (1,Leaf,Leaf))))

> isMemberOf 3 t;;
val it : bool = true
> isMemberOf 13 t;;
val it : bool = false
```

One problem with the unbalanced tree defined till now is that the worst case complexity of the *isMemberOf* operation is $O(n)$, where n is the cardinality of the set. We can address the performance by ordering the nodes in the tree. We will add some conditions in the insert function so all the labels in the left child are smaller than x for Node(x, left, right) and all the labels in the right side are greater than x. The modified insert function is as follows:

```
let rec insert x = function
    | Leaf -> Node(x, Leaf, Leaf)
    | Node(y, left, right) as node ->
        if x < y
        then Node(y, insert x left, right)
        else if x > y
        then Node(y, left, insert x right)
        else node

> let t = ofList [9; 11; 19; 4; 2; 1; 0];;
val t : int tree =
  Node
    (0,Leaf,
    Node
       (1,Leaf,
       Node
          (2,Leaf,
          Node (4,Leaf,Node (19,Node (11,Node
(9,Leaf,Leaf),Leaf),Leaf)))))
```

So now, with the data inserted in an ordered fashion, we can modify the `isMemberOf` function as shown in the following block of code:

```
let rec isMemberOf x t =
  | Leaf -> false
  | Node(y, left, right) ->
      x = y || (x < y && isMemberOf x left) || (x > y && isMemberOf x
right)

> isMemberOf 10 x;;
val it : bool = false
> isMemberOf 1 x;;
val it : bool = true
```

The complexity of this function is now *O(l)*, where *l* is the maximal depth of the tree. As the `insert` function still does not guarantee balancing, the complexity is still *O(n)* in the worst case.

Balanced red-black trees

In order to address the performance problem, we will implement a functional red-black tree. Red-black trees add a label, either red or black to each non-leaf node. The conditions for that are as follows:

- Every leaf is colored black
- All children of every red node are black
- Every path from the root to a leaf has the same number of black nodes as every other path
- The root is always black

As all the children of a red node are black and each path from the root to a leaf has the same number of black nodes, the longest path is at most twice as long as the shortest path. The structure definition of `rbtree` is defined as follows:

```
type color =
    | Red
    | Black

type 'a rbtree =
    | Leaf
    | Node of color * 'a * 'a rbtree * 'a rbtree
```

The difficult part of the data structure is to maintain the structure when a new value is inserted into the tree. In the following block of code, we will introduce a `balance` function that will adjust the tree to have proper balancing:

```
let balance = function
    | Black, z, Node(Red, y, Node(Red, x, a, b), c), d
    | Black, z, Node(Red, x, a, Node(Red, y, b, c)), d
    | Black, x, a, Node(Red, z, Node(Red, y, b, c), d)
    | Black, x, a, Node(Red, y, b, Node(Red, z, c, d)) ->
        Node(Red, y, Node(Black, x, a, b), Node(Black, z, c, d))
    | a, b, c, d ->
        Node(a, b, c, d)

let insert x s =
    let rec ins = function
        | Leaf -> Node(Red, x, Leaf, Leaf)
        | Node(color, y, a, b) as s ->
            if x < y then balance (color, y, ins a, b)
            else if x > y then balance (color, y, a, ins b)
            else s
    match ins s with
    | Node(_, y, a, b) -> Node(Black, y, a, b)
    | Leaf -> raise (System.InvalidOperationException())
```

Note the use of nested patterns in the `balance` function. The `balance` function takes a 4-tuple with a color, two b-trees, and an element and it splits the analysis into five cases; four of the cases are for the situation where the second condition needs to be re-established because `Red` nodes are nested, and the final case is when the tree does not need rebalancing.

As the longest path from the root is, at most, twice as long as the shortest path, the depth of the tree is *O(log n)*. The balance function takes *O(1)* time; this means the `insert` and `isMemberOf` function can take `O(log n)`:

```
let ofList t =
    let rec _ofList = function
        | [] -> empty
        | h :: t -> insert h (_ofList t)
    _ofList t

let isMemberOf x t =
    let rec mem x = function
        | Leaf -> false
        | Node(_, y, left, right) ->
            x = y || (x < y && mem x left) || (x > y && mem x right)

    mem x t
```

```
> let x = ofList [3;9;7;5;11];;

val x : int rbtree =
  Node
    (Black,7,Node (Black,5,Node (Red,3,Leaf,Leaf),Leaf),
     Node (Black,11,Node (Red,9,Leaf,Leaf),Leaf))
```

As we can see in the preceding piece of code, the nodes are now balanced and the performance is *O(log n)* with the red-black tree.

Summary

In this chapter, we were able to go through the main collections in the `FSharp.Core` library, such as lazy sequences, arrays, lists, maps, and sets; learned the difference between them in terms of mutability and memory and computation efficiency. We also saw how to use the functions in their respective modules to easily manipulate them.

After that, we worked with some advanced data structures that we coded ourselves, such as binary trees or balanced red-black trees. In the next chapter, we will go through the imperative constructs present in F#, and we will compare them with those in C#.

4
Imperative Programming in F#

In this chapter, you will learn how to use control structures, more idiomatic .NET with F#, interfacing with C#, and generics. The following are the topics that we will cover:

- Working with classes
- Control structures
- Operator overloading
- Interoperating with C#
- Extension methods
- Using LINQ in F#

As a developer, we also need to think of exposing functionalities from F# libraries to be used with C# or other .NET languages. In a team, not every member will be using F# and because of that, we will write wrapper functionalities or expose the F# code in a way that's more consumable in C#. And sometimes, mutable code inside of F# is used for performance-oriented programs; just like we discussed in the previous chapter, in some cases, not all data structures can be used in an immutable way because of memory and performance. And we will resort to using imperative ways to deal with such scenarios.

Control structures

Control structures refer to the decisions made that affect the order of execution of the code. Although F# is an expression-based language, it also provides control flow constructs common of statement-based languages, such as *looping*, that allows us to write code with side-effects. We will be discussing this, as well as how to express *conditions*, in the following sections.

Looping

There are two types of loops: the `for` loop and the `while` loop. The `For` loops have the following two types of expression:

- `for...to`: This iterates over a range of values
- `for...in`: This is more like the `foreach` loop in other .NET languages as it loops over an enumerable collection

The for...to expression

The `for...to` expression loops/iterates over a range of values. The range can be forward/reverse or generated via a function. The return of this expression is `unit` type.

The forward expression works by incrementing the following values in the loop:

```
// A simple for...to loop.
let function1() =
    for i = 1 to 10 do
        printf "%d " i
> 1 2 3 4 5 6 7 8 9 10
```

The reverse expression works by decrementing the following values in the loop:

```
// A for...to loop that counts in reverse.
let function2() =
    for i = 10 downto 1 do
        printf "%d " i
> 10 9 8 7 6 5 4 3 2 1
```

We can also use functions to determine the start and end value in the loop, as follows:

```
// A for...to loop that uses functions as the start and finish
expressions.
let beginning x y = x - 2*y
let ending x y = x + 2*y

let function3 x y =
    for i = (beginning x y) to (ending x y) do
        printf "%d " i
> -9 -8 -7 -6 -5 -4 -3 -2 -1 0 1 2 3 4 5 6 7 8 9 10 11
```

The for...in expression

The for...in expression is used to iterate over an enumerable collection. The return of this expression is unit type:

```
let function1() =
    for i in [4; -1; 3; 6] do
        printf "%d " i
> 4 -1 3 6
```

The preceding function iterates over the list and prints it. This is like the foreach loop we have in C#. In F#, we won't be able to use the yield keyword inside a for...in loop—the yield keyword is available only with sequence expressions in F#.

We can also use a mutable variable inside the for...in body expression. In the following example, we will do a count of the list:

```
let function2() =
    let mutable count = 0
    for _ in [1..10] do
        count <- count + 1
        printfn "Number of elements in list1: %d" count
> Number of elements in list1: 10
```

The while...do expression

The while loop is used to perform iteration as long as a specified condition is true. The test expression is evaluated, and if it is true, then the body expression is evaluated; the evaluation continues till the test expression returns false. The following example illustrates the use of the while...do loop:

```
let function1() =
    let mutable r = true
    let mutable c = 0
    while r do
        if c < 10 then
            c <- c + 1
        else
            r <- false
    printfn "counter value: %d" c
> counter value: 10
```

Conditions

The `If...then...else` construct is used to write conditional branching in F#; there is also `else if`, or `elif`, which we can use for multiple conditions:

```
let sizeToLabel (size: int): string =
    let label =
        if size < 10
        then "XS"
        elif size < 20
        then "S"
        elif size < 30
        then "M"
        elif size < 40
        then "L"
        else "XL"
    label
```

There is no `switch...case` statement; we will use pattern matching instead.

The scope for an `if` statement extends to any code indented under it.

When coming from language with a C-like syntax, it is often surprising that all branches of `if...then...else` must return a value of the same type. This can be compared to the conditional ternary operator (`?:`) present in other languages such as C# or JavaScript. However, when we want to test a condition to produce a side-effect, and the `then` branch returns the `unit` value, which is equivalent to a statement in other languages, the `else` branch can be omitted:

```
if error <> null then
    printfn "An error has occurred: %s" error
```

Working with conditions

F# has three Boolean operators, which are as follows:

- `&&`: Logical **AND**

  true && false = false

- | |: Logical **OR**

  true | | *false* = *true*

- not: Logical **Not**

  not false = *true*

The not operator is different than other .NET languages because it is a function rather than an operator. The following piece of code is an example showing its usage:

```
let x = 20
if not (x < 10) then
    printfn "x is greater than 10"
```

And as not is a function, we can use it just like any other F# function. The following is an example showing how to use the not operator with the F# List.map function:

```
let x_is_less_ten(x) = if x < 10 then true else false
[1..10] |> List.map(x_is_less_ten >> not)
val it : bool list =
    [false; false; false; false; false; false; false; false; false;
true]
```

Object-oriented programming

F# provides **object-oriented programming (OOP)** with relative ease. It is a first class functional language, as we have seen up until now and a first class OOP language as well. To be able to mix both the paradigms is a very powerful tool. We can easily extend .NET types that were implemented in other languages easily with F#. The main features of OOP are as follows:

- **Encapsulation:** Objects can hide information (code and data) about themselves to prevent unexpected modifications from other objects
- **Inheritance:** The definition of one type of object (a class) can be reused by a new definition that inherits the methods from the former class (its parent) and can extend them
- **Polymorphism:** Methods expecting arguments of a certain class can also accept descendants of that class

Defining a class

The simplest form of a class definition looks like a definition of an object with the following keyword:

```
type <class name><constructor arguments> =
    [class]
    <class body>
    [end]
```

 The `class` and `end` keywords are optional; they are only necessary if the class body is empty.

So, with this, we can define a simple class `Point` as follows:

```
type Point(x, y) =
    member this.X = x
    member this.Y = y

    override this.ToString() =
        sprintf "Point %s, %s" x y
```

We can instantiate the class using the following `let` definition:

```
> let p = new Point(10, 20);;
val p : Point = Point 10, 20
```

If we break a class into different parts, then we can see the following definitions:

- The class has a constructor accepting two variables
- The class defines two properties, `X` and `Y`
- The class overrides a `ToString` function from the base class

Let's take a look at the C# implementation of the same class:

```
public class Point
    {
        public Point(int x, int y)
        {
            this.X = x;
            this.Y = y;
        }
        public int X { get; private set; }
        public int Y { get; private set; }
```

```
public override string ToString()
{
    return String.Format("Point {0}, {1}", this.X, this.Y);
}
}
```

In the preceding code, there is certain differences that we can note:

- The F# constructor is directly in the type declaration
- Parameters in the F# constructor automatically become immutable private fields
- The F# syntax is much terser than the C# counterpart

Constructors

Constructors are nothing but additional functions in the class definition that accept initial values of the object. The following are the two ways we can define a constructor in F#:

- **Primary constructor**: This appears immediately after the type definition
- **Additional constructor**: This is the optional way to define additional constructors using the `new` keyword

The default constructor initializes all the fields to a default value for that type. Any other constructor must have a parameter signature that does not conflict with the default constructor, as follows:

```
type Point2(x0, y0) =
    let mutable x = x0
    let mutable y = y0

    member this.X with get() = x
                  and set(v) = x <- v

    member this.Y with get() = y
                  and set(v) = y <- v

    new() = Point2(0, 0)

    override this.ToString() =
        sprintf "Point %d, %d" x y
```

Note that X and Y are .NET properties. We will see these properties in detail in the following section.

In F#, there is no `this` keyword; every method or property must define a self identifier right before the method name. The preceding code uses `this`, but the F# compiler will accept any other valid identifier.

We can also define a `self` identifier in the constructor using the `as` clause right after the constructor parameters. For example, we may want to modify a property inherited from a super class:

```
type Parent () =
    let mutable v0 = 10

    member this.Value
        with get () = v0
        and set (v) = v0 <- v

type Child() as this =
    inherit Parent ()
    do this.Value <- 20

    override this.ToString () =
        sprintf "%i" this.Value
```

We will use the `do` keyword to execute some side-effect code inside the constructor in the following snippet:

```
type Person(nameIn : string, idIn : int) =
    let mutable name = nameIn
    let mutable id = idIn
    do printfn "Created a person object."
    member this.Name with get () = name and set (v) = name <- v
    member this.ID with get () = id and set (v) = id <- v
    new () =
        Person("Invalid Name", -1)
        then
            printfn "Created an invalid person object."
```

For additional constructors, we must use the `then` keyword.

Structs

Class instances in F#, as in other .NET languages, are just references; this means that the memory necessary to contain the data of the object is dynamically reserved by .NET runtime in an area known as the heap to which we only have indirect access through the references. When a copy of the reference is created (for example, with a let binding: `let myCopy = myObject`), we will end up with just two references to the same memory space. The .NET runtime also takes care of releasing that memory space when there are no more references available pointing at it (a process commonly known as garbage collection).

Sometimes, for performance reasons, we want to have more control of the memory of the object. In .NET, this is achieved with structures (or structs). Struct instances are not just references; they contain the whole data of the object in a memory location as the stack. The stack is a small memory space that is assigned to each function execution, and it is much faster than the heap. Another important difference with classes is that when we make a copy of the struct, we do actually copy all the data, so any change to the latter will not affect the former.

Structures are usually referred with the `type struct` construct. The fields are declared using the `val` keyword. If a field is defined by the `val` keyword, either in class or struct, it has to be initialized or set in the constructor:

```
type MyStruct =
    struct
        val X : int
        val Y : int
        val Z : int
        new(x, y, z) = { X = x; Y = y; Z = z }
    end

let myStructure1 = new MyStruct(1, 2, 3)
```

More information on the `val` keyword, which is also called an explicit field, is given in the next section.

Declaring fields, properties, methods, and static methods

In this topic, we will try to understand how to define field, properties, methods, and static methods inside a class. We will also look at different aspects in terms of F# and extensibilities available for these object-oriented functionalities.

Fields

Fields can be defined with the `let` binding with `private` access modifier. The syntax is similar as we use it outside the class; F# will simply treat any `let` binding variable as a private field inside a class. We can also declare a field mutable with the `mutable` keyword:

```
type PrivateFieldExample() =
    let mutable value = 0

    member this.UpdateValue(v) =
        value <- v
> let p = new PrivateFieldExample();;

val p : PrivateFieldExample

> p.UpdateValue(10);;
val it : unit = ()
```

The preceding example shows how we can declare a mutable field and update its value with a function.

Explicit fields

The `val` keyword is used to declare a field in a class or structure, but without initializing it to a default value. The default value can also be initialized with the primary constructor. Explicit fields can be static or non-static. The access modifier can be `public`, `private`, or `internal`. By default, the access modifier is `public`. This differs from the `let` binding, as we saw earlier.

The `DefaultValue` attribute is required on explicit fields that have a primary constructor. One of the following types can support zero-initialization :

- A primitive type that has zero value
- A type that supports a null value, such as .NET reference types, discriminated unions, tuples, records, and so on
- A .NET value type
- A structure whose fields all support a default zero value

We will look at two examples in which we can use the `val` keyword. The first example shows a class with a primary constructor initializing the values of x and y properties, which is as follows:

```
type ExplicitFieldExample1 =
    val x : int
    val y : int

    override this.ToString() =
        sprintf "x - %d, y - %d" this.x this.y

    new(x0, y0) = { x = x0; y = y0 }

> let e1 = new ExplicitFieldExample1(10, 20);;

val e1 : ExplicitFieldExample1 = x - 10, y - 20

> e1.ToString();;
val it : string = "x - 10, y - 20"
```

The second example shows how to create mutable `val` fields and update them, as follows:

```
type ExplicitFieldExample2() =
    [<DefaultValue>] val mutable x : int
    [<DefaultValue>] val mutable y : int

    member this.Update(x0, y0) =
        this.x <- x0
        this.y <- y0

    override this.ToString() =
        sprintf "x - %d, y - %d" this.x this.y
> let e2 = new ExplicitFieldExample2();;

val e2 : ExplicitFieldExample2 = x - 0, y - 0

> e2.Update(10, 20);;
val it : unit = ()
> e2.ToString();;
val it : string = "x - 10, y - 20"
```

Properties

Properties represent a way to access or modify the state inside the object. We can declare properties in two ways: one in the explicit way, where we will specify the details, and the other way is to tell the F# compiler to automatically generate the getter/setter for the object. To declare a property, we will use the member keyword. The two ways of declaring a property are:

- To make a property read/write, define both get/set accessor
- To make a property read-only, just declare the get accessor

```
type PropertyExample() =
    let mutable value = 0
    member this.Value with get() = value
                      and set(v:int) = value <- v


    member val AutoValue = 0 with get, set
> let p = new PropertyExample();;
val p : PropertyExample
> p.Value <- 10;;
val it : unit = ()
> p.Value;;
val it : int = 10
> p.AutoValue <- 20;;
val it : unit = ()
> p.AutoValue;;
val it : int = 20
```

The preceding example shows both the implicit and explicit ways to declare properties. The difference with implicit property declaration is that we will use the val keyword with get/set. There is one notable behavior difference with auto-properties–they initialize the default values in the constructor of the class. Let's consider the following example, which shows that the RandomValue property is the same if we try to access it multiple times:

```
type PropertyExample2() =
    let r = new System.Random()
    member val RandomValue = r.NextDouble() with get, set

> let p = new PropertyExample2();;

val p : PropertyExample2

> p.RandomValue;;
val it : float = 0.3954316994
> p.RandomValue;;
```

```
val it : float = 0.3954316994
```

Static properties

All the properties we have seen so far are instance properties; this means that we will need an instance of the class to access them, and also each instance can produce different values. However, sometimes, we may need a single property for the whole type that can be accessed without having to instantiate the class; these are the `static` properties. Properties and fields can be declared static using the `static` keyword:

```
type MyStaticClass() =
    static let mutable myStaticValue = 5
    static member MyStaticProperty
        with get() = myStaticValue
        and set(value) = myStaticValue <- value

printfn "%i" MyStaticClass.MyStaticProperty
```

Indexed properties

Indexed properties allow array-like access to data. The syntax for an indexed property is as follows:

```
member self-identifier.PropertyName
   with get(index-variable) =
       get-function-body
   and set index-variables value-variables =
       set-function-body
```

Like other property types, we can also have a read-only or set-only indexed property. Let's consider the following block of code as an example:

```
type IndexedPropertyExample() =
    let numbers = [| 1..10 |]
    member this.Squares
        with get(i): float = float numbers.[i] ** 2.
        and set i (v: float) = numbers.[i] <- int(sqrt v)
    member this.Item
        with get(i) = numbers.[i]
        and set i v = numbers.[i] <- v

> let i = new IndexedPropertyExample();;
val i : IndexedPropertyExample

> i.[0];;
val it : int = 1
```

```
> i.[0] <- 20;;
val it : unit = ()
> i.[0];;
val it : int = 20
> i.Squares(2);;
val it: float = 9.
> i.Squares(2) <- 16.;;
val it: unit = ()
```

When the name of the indexed property is Item, the compiler treats it as a default indexed property, that is, it can be accessed without using the name of the property later on; we can also use square brackets as in C#, but note that the period is necessary before the brackets. When any name other than Item is used, the property is accessed by its name, and round brackets are used instead for the index.

We can modify the value using the indexer property and also get back the value from it. This is very similar to the way we declare in C# as well.

Multiple indexed properties

Indexed property with more than one index is also allowed. We can do it by declaring multiple keys in the get/set accessors, as follows:

```
let mutable table = new Dictionary<(int * int), float>()
    member this.Item
        with get(key1, key2) = table.[(key1, key2)]
        and set (key1, key2) value = table.[(key1, key2)] <- value
```

Methods

A method is a function associated to a type. In OOP, methods are used to expose and implement the functionality and behavior of the type. Methods are a declared part of the type with the member keyword and a self-identifier:

```
type MethodExample() =
    member this.PrintValue(s: string) =
        printf "%s" s
> let m = new MethodExample();;
val m : MethodExample
> m.PrintValue("Hello World");;
Hello World
```

Static methods

The `static` keyword is used to specify that a method can be called without an instance and is not associated with an object instance:

```
type MyStaticClass() =
    static member SomeStaticMethod(a, b, c) = (a + b + c)
MyStaticClass.SomeStaticMethod(1,2,3)
|> printfn "Result: %i"
```

Abstract and virtual methods

The `abstract` keyword is used to define a method as an abstract method. This typically means that it is not implemented in the class where it is defined, but in the inheriting class. Abstract methods don't have the method body, but the method declaration and the parameters for that. In F#, there is one difference, we can also create curried parameters using the arrow symbol (`->`), and if we want to have proper interoperability with C#, then we can declare the functions as tuples:

- A method definition with tuple parameters is as follows:

```
abstract member Add : int * int -> int
```

- A method definition with curried parameters is shown as follows:

```
abstract member Add : int -> int -> int
```

We will then use the `override` keyword to define the overridden method in the subclasses. We can also use the `default` keyword to define a default implementation of the method; this is used to define a virtual function in F#. It is a bit cumbersome to define two methods for a virtual method:

```
type BaseEmployeeObject(employeeId: int) =
    let mutable empId = employeeId

    abstract member GetEmployeeId : unit -> int
    default this.GetEmployeeId() = employeeId

type CEOEmployeeObject(employeeId) =
    inherit BaseEmployeeObject(employeeId)

    override this.GetEmployeeId() = 0
```

Overloaded methods are methods that have identical names in a given type, but those that have different arguments. In F#, optional arguments are usually used instead of overloaded methods:

```
type OverloadedExample() =
    member this.GetXY(x, y) =
        x * 2 + y * 2
    member this.GetXY(x) =
        this.GetXY(x, 0)

> let e = new OverloadedExample();;
val e : OverloadedExample
> e.GetXY(10,10);;
val it : int = 40
> e.GetXY(10);;
val it : int = 20
```

The preceding example shows that we can write overloaded methods just like in C#.

Parameters

Parameters are variables supplied to functions. Methods usually use the tuple form of passing arguments:

```
member this.Method1(param1, param2) =
```

The curried form is mostly used with the let bindings:

```
let function1 param1 param2 =
```

Combined forms are also possible, as seen in the following code snippet:

```
let function1 param1 (p2, p3) p4 =
```

We can also use a wildcard pattern when defining a parameter that we we don't want to use; let's consider the following line of code as an example:

```
let makeList _ = [ for i in 1 .. 10 -> i * i ]
let list1 = makeList 100
```

Sometimes, we can directly use pattern matching in the function parameter, as shown in the following line of code:

```
type Action = DoSomething of int * int
let computeAction (DoSomething(x, y)) = x * y
```

Named arguments

Arguments for methods can be specified by position in the comma-separated list, or they can be explicitly named:

```
type Calculator() =
member this.Subtract(minuend: int, subtrahend: int) =
minuend - subtrahend
> let calc = Calculator();;
> calc.Subtract(5, 3);;
val it : int = 2
> calc.Subtract(3, 5);;
val it : int = -2
> calc.Subtract(subtrahend=3, minuend=5);;
val it : int = 2
```

It is similar to the way we declare in C# by defining the type for all the variables in methods, constructors, or properties.

Optional parameters

You can specify an optional parameter for a method using a question mark in front of the parameter name, as follows:

```
type Employee(employeeId: int, ?employeeName: string) =
    member this.EmployeeName = defaultArg employeeName "Karl"

let emp1 = new Employee(100, employeeName = "John")
let emp2 = new Employee(101, "Smith")
let emp3 = new Employee(102)
> emp3.EmployeeName;;
val it: string = "Karl"
```

This is also similar to the C# way of defining optional parameters. However, in C#, we will need to provide a default value for the case when the calling code omits the argument. Whereas, in F#, within the body of the function, the actual type of the argument is an option type. To access the value, we will often use defaultArg, which just does pattern matching against the option and returns a default value if it is None:

```
let defaultArg (arg: 'T option) (defaultValue: 'T): 'T =
    match arg with
    | Some value -> value
    | None -> defaultValue
```

Inheritance

Inheritanc is the ability to define new classes by reusing an existing class. .NET only allows single e is the ability to define new classes by reusing an existing class. .NET only allows single inheritance, that is, a class can only have one parent. We can declare abstract classes, define interfaces, or have overriding methods that are useful to abstract code in an object-oriented way.

Use the `inherit` keyword to inherit from another class:

```
type BaseEmployee(empId: int) =
    member x.EmployeeId = empId

type SupervisorEmployee(superVisorId:int, empId: int) =
    inherit BaseEmployee(empId)

    member x.SuperVisorId = superVisorId
```

The preceding example defines two classes: `BaseEmployee` and `SuperVisorEmployee`, and uses the `inherit` keyword to derive the latter from the former. If we initialize a `SupervisorEmployee` object, we will get back `EmployeeId` from the base class:

```
> let supervisor = new SupervisorEmployee(100, 10001);;

val supervisor : SupervisorEmployee

> supervisor.SuperVisorId;;
val it : int = 100
```

Abstract

Abstract classes or methods in .NET allow the developer to define abstract definitions of the object and derive to one or more subclasses. Any subclass implementing from an abstract class has to override all abstract methods or properties and define the implementation for it.

We can use the abstract keyword to define an abstract method. We will need to specially mark the class with the `<AbstractClass>` attribute to make the class an abstract class:

```
[<AbstractClass>]
type BaseEmployee2(empId: int) =
    member x.EmployeeId = empId
    abstract member GetDesination : unit -> string
// abstract read/write property
    abstract member Age : int with get,set
```

To implement an abstract class, we can inherit the abstract class and override the abstract methods or properties. The following heading is a given example.

Defining an interface

An interface is defined similar to a class except the member definitions are marked as abstract. The `interface` and `end` keywords, which mark the start and end of the definition, are optional when you use lightweight syntax. If you do not use these keywords, the compiler attempts to infer whether the type is a class or an interface by analyzing the constructs that you use. If you define a member or use other class syntax, the type is interpreted as a class:

```
type ICalculator =
    interface
        abstract member Add : int * int -> int
        abstract member Subract : int * int -> int
    end

type Calculator =
    interface ICalculator with
        member this.Add(x, y) = x + y
        member this.Subract(x, y) = x - y
```

The preceding code defines an `ICalculator` interface with two methods defined with their function parameters. Just like a .NET interface, all the methods defined are public and must be implemented in a class.

Implement interface in F# types

F# records allow implementing an interface, but they cannot be inherited. Simply indent and write the implementation of the interface just like an F# class, and it should be available for use. The following class implements the `System.IDisposable` interface:

```
type EmployeeList =
    {
        Employees : List<Employee>
    }
        interface System.IDisposable with
            member x.Dispose() =
                // write dispose code here
                x.Employees.Clear()
> let empList = Employee.Get(departmentID);; //some DB call to fetch
employees
```

```
> (empList :> System.IDisposable).Dispose();; //dispose the object
```

In F#, any type can't directly access the interface methods or properties. We can use the :> operator to cast up from the type to the implemented interface and use the object. We can also use the upcast keyword to do the same operation.

In F#, we can also define an interface using a let binding; it is called as implementing an interface using object expressions. This is useful when working with module functions or, sometimes, a small interface for which we don't have to declare a class separately:

```
module Calc =
    let get () =
        { new ICalculator with
            member this.Add(x, y) = x + y
            member this.Subract(x, y) = x - y }
```

Interface inheritance

Interfaces can also inherit from one or more base interface. Let's consider the following example:

```
type Interface1 =
    abstract member Method1 : int -> int

type Interface2 =
    abstract member Method2 : int -> int

type Interface3 =
    inherit Interface1
    inherit Interface2
    abstract member Method3 : int -> int

type MyClass() =
    interface Interface3 with
        member this.Method1(n) = 2 * n
        member this.Method2(n) = n + 100
        member this.Method3(n) = n / 10
```

Extensions

Extensions are syntactic sugar that allow writing new members to an existing type. There are two forms of extensions that we can define: an **intrinsic** extension is an extension that appears in the same namespace or module and in the same assembly, and an **optional** extension is an extension that appears in a different module or namespace and assembly.

An example of the intrinsic extension is as follows:

```
module MyModule1 =

    // Define a type.
    type Calculator() =
      member this.Add(x, y) = x + y

    // Define type extension.
    type Calculator with
        member this.Mult(x, y) = x * y

module MyModule2 =
    let function1 (obj1: MyModule1.Calculator) =
        // Call an ordinary method.
        printfn "%d" (obj1.Add(10, 20))
        // Call the extension method.
        printfn "%d" (obj1.Mult(10, 20))
```

The optional extension can be defined to existing types; let's consider the following piece of code, for example:

```
// Define a new member method FromString on the type Int32.
type System.Int32 with
    member this.ToDouble() =
        this |> float

let x = 10
  let i = x.ToDouble()
printfn "%f" i
```

Generics

F# functions, discriminated unions, records, and object-oriented style expressions can be generic. Generics are a very intrinsic part of F#. Making your code generic can be simple in F# because your code is often implicitly inferred to be generic by the compiler's type inference and automatic generalization mechanisms.

For an explicit generic function or type, we will need to declare the generic type as <'T> using angle brackets, just like in C#.

```
type Calculator<'T>
or
member this.Add<'T>('T x, 'T y)
```

An important difference with C# is that, in F#, we will need to prefix the name of the compiler arguments with an apostrophe.

Implicit declarations, as said, are inferred automatically by the F# compiler. So basically, we can define the function or the type, and that's it:

```
let add x y = x + y
or
member this.Add(x, y) = x + y
```

There are some limitations with automatic generalizations; for example, if the F# compiler may not be able to generalize a generic construct, the compiler will report an error for that, so we will need to add generic type annotations in this case.

Using generic constructs

When using generic constructs, we don't have to specifically define the type we are using. Again, the compiler will infer from the type we are declaring.

```
// In this case, the type argument is inferred to be int.
function1 10 20
// In this case, the type argument is float.
function1 10.0 20.0
```

Wildcard generic constructs

We can also use wildcards such as seq<_> instead of typed argument. An example code is as follows:

```
let printSequence (sequence1: Collections.seq<_>) =
    Seq.iter (fun elem -> printf "%s " (elem.ToString())) sequence1
```

Generic constraints

In a generic type or function definition, you can use only those constructs that are known to be available on the generic type parameter. This is required to enable the verification of function and method calls at compile time. There are several different constraints that we can apply to limit the types that can be used in a generic type.

Constraint	Syntax	Description
Type constraint	`type-parameter :> type`	Provided type must be equal or a derived type
Null constraint	`type-parameter: null`	Provided type must support null literal
Explicit member constraint	`[type-parameter]: (member-signature)`	At least one of the type arguments provided must have a member that has a specified signature
Constructor constraint	`type-parameter: (new : unit -> 'a)`	Provided type must have a default constructor
Value type constraint	`: struct`	Provided type is a .NET value type
Reference type constraint	`: not struct`	Provided type must be a .NET reference type
Enumeration type constraint	`: enum<type>`	Provided type must be an enumerated type
Delegate constraint	`: delegate<tuple-parameter, return type>`	Provided type must be a delegate type with specified arguments and return type.
Comparison constraint	`: comparison`	Provided type must support comparison
Equality constraint	`: equality`	Provided type must support equality
Unmanaged constraint	`: unmanaged`	Provided type must be unmanaged type

The following example types show all the different constraint types:

```
// Base Type Constraint
type TypeConstraintExample<'T when 'T :> System.IDisposable> =
    class end

// Null constraint
type MyOwnClass<'T when 'T : null> =
    class end

// Member constraint with static member
type MemberConstraint<'T when 'T : (static member MyFunction : unit ->
```

```
'T) > =
        class end

    // Member constraint with property
    type PropertyConstraint<'T when 'T : (member EmployeeId : int)> =
        class end

    // Constructor constraint
    type ConstructorConstraint<'T when 'T : (new : unit -> 'T)>() =
        member val Field = new 'T()

    // Reference type constraint
    type ReferenceType<'T when 'T : not struct> =
        class end

    // Enumeration constraint with underlying value specified
    type EnumTypeConstraint<'T when 'T : enum<uint32>> =
        class end

    // 'T must implement IComparable, or be an array type with comparable
    // elements, or be System.IntPtr or System.UIntPtr. Also, 'T must not
have
    // the NoComparison attribute.
    type MyComparerType<'T when 'T : comparison> =
        class end

    // 'T must support equality. This is true for any type that does not
    // have the NoEquality attribute.
    type MyEqualityType<'T when 'T : equality> =
        class end

    // 'T must be a delegate type with the specified signature
    type MyDelegateType<'T when 'T : delegate<obj * System.EventArgs,
unit>> =
        class end

    // 'T must be an unmanaged type
    type MyUnmanagedType<'T when 'T : unmanaged> =
        class end
```

Generic extensions

Generic extensions are a new feature in F#, introduced in the F# 3.1 compiler:

```
    type seq<'T> with
        /// Repeat each element of the sequence n times
```

```
member xs.RepeatElements(n: int) =
    seq { for x in xs do for i in 1 .. n do yield x }
```

Using LINQ in F#

F# has query expressions that help to easily build **Language Integrated Query (LINQ)** queries. Query expressions can be declared as query { ... }. It is a type of computation expression, just like the sequence expression. An example code is given as follows:

```
let data = [| 1..10 |]

let simpleExpression() =
    query {
        for d in data do
        select d
        contains 5
    }
> simpleExpression();;
val it : bool = true
```

Query expressions have a list of query operators with which we can use the LINQ-like operations on the data:

```
let designations = [| "CEO"; "CTO"; "Manager"; "Employee" |]

type Employee =
    {
        FirstName: string
        LastName: string
        Designation: string
        Salary: int
    } with
        static member DummyData() =
            let r = new System.Random()
            seq {
                for i = 0 to 10 do
                    let e = {
                        FirstName = sprintf "FirstName%d" i
                        LastName = sprintf "LastName%d" i
                        Designation =
designations.[r.Next(designations.Length-1)]
                        Salary = r.Next(10000)
                    }
                    yield e
            }
            |> Seq.toArray
```

Note that, for the purpose of examples, we will assume that we have a list employee records with `FirstName`, `LastName`, `Designation`, and `Salary` fields.

The following are the lists of operators that are supported in a query expression:

Operator	Description

contains	This checks if the data has the element:
	``query {
	    for e in Employee.DummyData() do
	    select e.Designation
	    contains "CEO"
	}```

count	This returns the number of elements:
	``query {
	    for e in Employee.DummyData() do
	    select e
	    count
	}```

last	This selects the last element in the sequence:
	``query {
	    for e in Employee.DummyData() do
	    select e
	    last
	}```

lastOrDefault	This selects the last element, if it's there in the sequence, or the default value for the type:
	``query {
	    for e in Employee.DummyData() do
	    select e
	    lastOrDefault
	}```

exactlyOne	This selects the single, specific element from the sequence:
	``query {
	    for e in Employee.DummyData() do
	    where (e.Designation = "CEO")
	    select e
	    exactlyOne
	}```

exactlyOneOrDefault	This selects the single, specific element from the sequence, or the default value for the type:
	``
	query {
	    for e in Employee.DummyData() do
	    where (e.Designation = "CEO")
	    select e
	    exactlyOneOrDefault
	}
	``

head	This selects the first element in the sequence:
	``
	query {
	    for numbers in data do
	    head
	}
	``

headOrDefault	This selects the first element or the default value for the type:
	``
	query {
	    for e in Employee.DummyData() do
	    where (e.Designation = "CEO")
	    select e
	    headOrDefault
	}
	``

select	This is the projection to select from the sequence:
	``
	query {
	    for e in Employee.DummyData() do
	    select e.FirstName, e.Designation
	}
	``

where	This selects elements based on a predicate:
	``
	query {
	    for e in Employee.DummyData() do
	    where (e.Designation = "CEO")
	    select e
	}
	``

minBy	This selects a value that's the minimum from the sequence:
	``
	query {
	    for e in Employee.DummyData() do
	    select e
	    minBy e.Salary
	}
	``

`minByNullable`	This selects a value that's the minimum from the sequence of the nullable property: ```query {\n for e in Employee.DummyData() do\n select e\n minByNullable e.Salary\n }```
`maxBy`	This selects a value that's the maximum from the sequence: ```query {\n for e in Employee.DummyData() do\n select e\n maxBy e.Salary\n }```
`maxByNullable`	This selects a value that's the maximum from the sequence of the nullable property: ```query {\n for e in Employee.DummyData() do\n select e\n maxByNullable e.Salary\n}```
`groupBy`	This groups the elements based on the specified key selector: ```query {\n for e in Employee.DummyData() do\n groupBy e.Designation into g\n select (g.Key, g.Count())\n }```
`sortBy`	This sorts the elements in ascending order by the given sort key: ```query {\n for e in Employee.DummyData() do\n sortBy e.Designation\n select e\n }```
`sortByDescending`	This sorts the elements in descending order by the given sort key: ```query {\n for e in Employee.DummyData() do\n sortByDescending e.Designation\n select e\n }```

thenBy	This performs a subsequent ordering of elements in ascending order; it can be used after `sortBy`, `sortByDescending`, `thenBy`, or `thenByDescending`: ```query { for e in Employee.DummyData() do sortBy e.Designation thenBy e.Salary select e }```
thenByDescending	This performs a subsequent ordering of elements in descending order; it can be used after a `sortBy`, `sortByDescending`, `thenBy`, or `thenByDescending`: ```query { for e in Employee.DummyData() do sortBy e.Designation thenByDescending e.Salary select e }```
sortByNullable	This sorts the elements in ascending order by the given nullable sort key: ```query { for e in Employee.DummyData() do sortByNullable e.Designation select e }```
sortByNullableDescending	This sorts the elements in descending order by the given nullable sort key: ```query { for e in Employee.DummyData() do sortByNullableDescending e.Designation select e }```
thenByNullable	This performs a subsequent ordering of elements in ascending order with a nullable sort key; it can be used after `sortBy`, `sortByDescending`, `thenBy`, or `thenByDescending`: ```query { for e in Employee.DummyData() do sortBy e.Designation thenByNullable e.Salary select e }```

`thenByNullableDescending`	This performs a subsequent ordering of elements in descending order with a nullable sort key; it can be used after `sortBy`, `sortByDescending`, `thenBy` or `thenByDescending`: ```\nquery {\n for e in Employee.DummyData() do\n sortBy e.Designation\n thenByNullableDescending e.Salary\n select e\n}\n```
`groupValBy`	This selects a value for each element selected so far and groups the element with the given key: ```\nquery {\n for e in Employee.DummyData() do\n groupValBy e.Designation e.Salary into g\n select (g, g.Key, g.Count())\n}\n```
`join`	This correlates two sets based on matching keys: ```\nquery { for e in Employee.DummyData() do\n join empDetails in EmployeeDetails.DummyData()\non\n (e.EmployeeID = empDetails.EmployeeID)\n select (e, empDetails)\n}\n```
`averageByNullable`	This selects a value for each element selected so far and returns the average of these values from nullable property: ```\nquery {\n for e in Employee.DummyData() do\n averageByNullable e.Salary\n}\n```
`averageBy`	This selects a value for each element selected so far and returns the average of these values: ```\nquery {\n for e in Employee.DummyData() do\n averageBy e.Salary\n}\n```
`distinct`	This selects the distinct elements so far: ```\nquery { for e in Employee.DummyData() do\n join empDetails in\n EmployeeDetails.DummyData() on\n (e.EmployeeID = empDetails.EmployeeID)\n distinct\n}\n```

exists	This determines whether any element selected so far satisfies a condition:
	
	``
	query {
	    for e in Employee.DummyData() do
	    where
	       (query {
	          for courseSelec in
	           Employee.CourseSelection do
	          exists (courseSelec.EmployeeID =
	          e.EmployeeID) })
	       select student
	}
	``

find	This selects the first element selected so far that satisfies a specified condition:
	
	``
	query {
	        for e in Employee.DummyData() do
	        find (e.Designation = "CEO")
	        select e
	}
	``

all	This determines if all the elements in the sequence satisfies a condition:
	
	``
	query {
	        for emp in Employee.DummyData() do
	        all (SqlMethods.Like(emp.Name, "%,%"))
	}
	``

nth	This selects the element at the specified index:
	
	``
	query {
	        for numbers in data do
	        nth 3
	}
	``

sumBy	This selects a value and returns the sum for the elements:
	
	``
	query {
	        for e in Employee.DummyData() do
	        sumBy e.Salary
	}
	``

sumByNullable	This selects a value and returns the sum for the elements from a nullable property:
	
	``
	query {
	        for e in Employee.DummyData() do
	        sumByNullable e.Salary
	}
	``

skip	This skips the specified number of elements from the sequence and returns the elements:
	
	``
	query { for i = 0 to 100 do
	   select i
	   skip 10
	
	}
	``

skipWhile	This skips the specified number of elements from the sequence till the condition is true and returns the elements:
	
	``
	query {
	   for i = 0 to 100 do
	   select i
	   skipWhile (i < 10)
	   }
	``

take	This selects the elements in the sequence until the condition is true:
	
	``
	query { for i = 0 to 100 do
	   select i
	   take 10
	   }
	``

takeWhile	This selects the elements in the sequence until the condition is true:
	
	``
	query { for i = 0 to 100 do
	   takeWhile (i < 50)
	   }
	``

Events

Events are basically callbacks from GUI elements that allow us to write custom user actions. When using a GUI library, such as Windows Forms or **Windows Presentation Foundation (WPF)**, events are part of the GUI classes. We can add custom behavior by adding a listener to these events. For example, if we want to handle the click event of a button in a login form, we can write a listener code for the `Click` event of that **Login** button.

Events in F# are first-class citizens, which means that they are exposed as a type `IEvent<'T>` that are composable using the `Events` module. Let's take a look at declaring events and using them, and then dive into using event processing in GUI programming.

Declaring events

Events are created using the F# `Event<'T>` class, which is a wrapper implementation around the .NET eventing system. It has the following two functions:

- `Publish`: This is used to expose the event
- `Trigger`: This triggers or raises the event with the arguments

The following piece of code is an example where we will implement an `INotifyPropertyChanged` interface, which is mostly used in WPF for data-binding scenarios:

```
open System.ComponentModel
type Employee() =
    let mutable firstName = ""
    let mutable lastName = ""

    let event = Event<_, _>()

    interface INotifyPropertyChanged with
        [<CLIEvent>]
        member this.PropertyChanged = event.Publish
    member this.FirstName with get() = firstName
                          and set(v) =
                                firstName <- v
                                this.OnPropertyChanged("FirstName")

    member this.LastName with get() = lastName
                         and set(v) =
                                lastName <- v
                                this.OnPropertyChanged("LastName")

    member this.OnPropertyChanged(propertyName) =
        event.Trigger(this, new PropertyChangedEventArgs(propertyName))
```

The preceding code sample performs:

- Event declaration using generic type, which automatically gets resolved based on the usage
- Implements an interface with event handler
- Triggers an event when property values are changed

It is very easy to add callbacks to the event handlers:

```
> let emp = new Employee();;
val emp : Employee
(emp :> INotifyPropertyChanged).PropertyChanged.AddHandler(fun _ e ->
    printfn "property changed - %s" e.PropertyName
);;
> emp.FirstName <- "Sarah";;
property changed - FirstName
> emp.LastName <- "Peterson";;
property changed - LastName
```

 When multiple callbacks are added to event handlers, they will be called in the order of the sequence they were used in the code.

Event processing

Event processing allows writing composable code with functions and writing high-level functions to drive the events. We have already seen how we can use `Seq`, `List`, or `Array` in composable functions using the several functions that these modules provide. Likewise, events can also be composed using the `Event` module; here is a list of functions that are available:

- `Event.add`: This adds a handler to the incoming event. This returns a `unit` type.
- `Event.map`: This returns a new event that fires on a selection of messages from the original event. The selector function returns a new message.
- `Event.choose`: This selector takes an original message and returns a new optional message.
- `Event.filter`: This triggers the resulting event only when the argument passed passes the function predicate.
- `Event.merge`: This fires the output of the event, if either of the events fire.
- `Event.pairwise`: This returns a new event that triggers on the second and subsequent triggering of the input event.
- `Event.partition`: This returns a new event that listens to the original event and triggers the first resulting event if the application of the predicate returned `true` for the first and `false` for the next event.
- `Event.scan`: This returns a new event consisting of the results of applying the given accumulating function to successive values triggered on the input event.

- Event.split: This returns a new event and triggers the first resulting event if the application of the function returns a Choice1Of2, and the second event if it returns Choice2Of2.

Let's look at an example with Windows Forms by drawing a circle and listening to the click event, as follows:

```
open System.Drawing
open System.Windows.Forms

// Generate random location for the ellipse
let rnd = new System.Random()
let x, y = rnd.Next(550), rnd.Next(350)

let dist (x1: int) (y1: int) (x2: int) (y2: int) =
    let distX = float(x2 - x1)
    let distY = float(y2 - y1)
    sqrt(distX ** 2. + distY ** 2.)

// Create the main form
let frm = new Form(ClientSize=Size(600,400))
// Add event handler to paint the ellipse
frm.Paint.Add(fun e ->
    e.Graphics.FillRectangle(Brushes.White, 0, 0, 600, 400)
    e.Graphics.FillEllipse(Brushes.DarkOliveGreen, x, y, 50, 50)
  )
frm.Show()

let leftMouseBtnClicks =
    frm.MouseDown
    |> Event.filter(fun e -> e.Button = MouseButtons.Left)

leftMouseBtnClicks.Add(fun e ->
    if dist e.X e.Y x y < 50. then
        MessageBox.Show("Left button clicked") |> ignore
)
```

The result of the preceding code snippet should look something like the following screenshot:

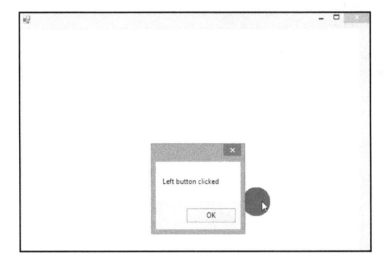

The sample uses `Event.filter` to filter out left clicks on the mouse button, and we will use that to process our own function handlers. Likewise, we can compose one or more events and write up functions that are easy to reason about, just like we do with lists, arrays, or sequences.

Declaring delegates

As we have seen, F# functions behave differently from other .NET languages as they can be partially applied. As a result, when we want to expose a function signature to other languages, we must use a **delegate**, which is the standard way to represent invokable objects in .NET. If we want to expose an event handler from F# to C#, or VB.NET, we can define a custom delegate type using the `delegate` keyword. The delegate is a type in itself, so we will need to declare it as follows:

```
type <typename> = delegate of args
```

The following piece of code is an example of the same `Employee` class with a custom delegate:

```
type MyPropertyChangedDelegate = delegate of obj *
PropertyChangedEventArgs
    -> unit

type EmployeeWithDelegate() =
    let mutable firstName = ""
```

```
        let mutable lastName = ""

        let event = Event<MyPropertyChangedDelegate,
PropertyChangedEventArgs>()

        [<CLIEvent>]
        member this.PropertyChanged = event.Publish
        member this.FirstName with get() = firstName
                            and set(v) =
                                firstName <- v
                                this.OnPropertyChanged("FirstName")

        member this.LastName with get() = lastName
                            and set(v) =
                                lastName <- v
                                this.OnPropertyChanged("LastName")

        member private this.OnPropertyChanged(propertyName) =
            event.Trigger(this, new PropertyChangedEventArgs(propertyName))
```

Observables

In .NET, the `IObservable` interface was introduced in the .NET 4.0 framework edition; basically, it is a generalized mechanism for push-based notifications, also known as the observer design pattern. The `IObservable<'T>` interface represents the class that sends notifications (provider) and the `IObserver<'T>` interface represents the class that receives from them (the observer). The provider must implement a single method, `Subscribe`, which indicates that an observer wants to receive push-based notifications. This method returns an `IDisposable` interface object that can be used to cancel observers any time before the provider has stopped sending them.

Observables are very similar to our F# first-class events, with the inheritance chain of `IEvent` from `IObservable` interface; it is possible to use the same combinations from event to observables. One advantage of using `IObservables` is that it returns an `IDisposable` object for a processing pipeline; this object can be used to dispose all the handlers that were wired up during the pipeline.

Similar to F# events, we can write composable functions using the following functions:

- `Observable.add`: This creates an observer that subscribes to the given observable and calls the function on every observation.
- `Observable.map`: This returns an observable that transforms the observables of the source by the given function.

- `Observable.choose`: This returns an observable that chooses a projection of observables from the source using the given function. The returned object will trigger observations when the projection returns some value.
- `Observable.filter`: This returns an observable that filters the observations of the source by the given function.
- `Observable.merge`: This returns an observable for the merged observations from the source.
- `Observable.pairwise`: This returns a new observable that triggers on the second and subsequent triggering of the input observable.
- `Observable.partition`: This returns two observables; the first trigger is for observations that returned `true`, and the second one is for `false`.
- `Observable.scan`: This returns an observable where each item is passed as an accumulated state to the successive functions as input.
- `Observable.split`: This returns two observables that split the observations of the source given by the function; the first will trigger observations, for which the splitter returns `Choice1Of2`, and the second will trigger, for which the splitter returns `Choice2Of2`.
- `Observable.subscribe`: This creates an observer that subscribes to the given observable and calls for each function. Additionally, this returns an `IDisposable` object that can be used to remove all the handlers when the `Dispose()` method is called.

We will walk through an example to showcase how to declare an `IObservable/IObserver` interface with F#. We will define an F# record, `Location`, that has `Latitude` and `Longitude` as properties:

```
type Location =
    {
        Latitude  : float
        Longitude : float
    }
```

The `LocationTracker` class provides the `IObservable<T>` implementation. Its `TrackLocation` method is passed a nullable `Location` object that contains the latitude and longitude data. The `TrackLocation` method calls the `OnNext` method of each observer:

```
type LocationTracker () =
    let observers = new List<IObserver<Location>>()

    member this.Subscribe(obs) =
```

```
        if observers.Contains(obs) |> not then
            observers.Add(obs)
        this.Unsubscriber(obs)

    member private this.Unsubscriber(obs) =
        { new System.IDisposable with
            member x.Dispose() =
                if observers.Contains(obs) then
                    observers.Remove(obs) |> ignore }

    member this.TrackLocation(location: Location) =
        observers
        |> Seq.iter(fun obs -> obs.OnNext(location))

    member this.EndTransmission() =
        observers
        |> Seq.iter(fun obs -> obs.OnCompleted())
        observers.Clear()

    interface System.IObservable<Location> with
        member x.Subscribe(obs) = x.Subscribe(obs)
```

Observers register to receive notifications from a `TrackLocation` object by calling its `IObservable<T>.Subscribe` method, which assigns a reference to the observer object to a private generic `List<T>` object. The method returns an `Unsubscriber` object, which is an `IDisposable` implementation that enables observers to stop receiving notifications. The `LocationTracker` class also includes an `EndTransmission` method. When no further location data is available, the method calls each observer's `OnCompleted` method and then clears the internal list of observers:

```
    type LocationReporter(instanceName) =
        let mutable dispObject : IDisposable = null

        member this.Name with get() = instanceName

        member this.Subscribe(provider: IObservable<Location>) =
            dispObject <- provider.Subscribe(this :> IObserver<Location>)

        member this.Unsubscribe() =
            if dispObject <> null then
                dispObject.Dispose()

        interface IObserver<Location> with
            member x.OnNext value   =
                printfn "Current location is %f, %f" value.Latitude
                    value.Longitude
```

```
member x.OnError ex     =
    printfn "Location cannot be determined"

member x.OnCompleted()  =
    printfn "Location tracker has completed transmission"
```

In the preceding example code, the `LocationReporter` class provides the `IObserver<T>` implementation. It displays information about the current location to the console. Its constructor includes a `name` parameter that enables the `LocationReporter` instance to identify itself in its string output. It also includes a `Subscribe` method that wraps a call to the provider's `Subscribe` method.

The following code instantiates the provider and reporter:

```
let provider = new LocationTracker()
let reporter1 = new LocationReporter("FixedGPS")
reporter1.Subscribe(provider)

let reporter2 = new LocationReporter("MobileGPS")
reporter2.Subscribe(provider)

provider.TrackLocation({ Latitude = 47.5678; Longitude = -100.11 })
reporter1.Unsubscribe()
provider.TrackLocation({ Latitude = 47.5678; Longitude = -100.11 })
provider.EndTransmission()
```

The output of the preceding code is as follows:

```
Current location is 47.567800, -100.110000
Current location is 47.567800, -100.110000
Current location is 47.567800, -100.110000
Location tracker has completed transmission
```

Interop with C#

Some F# features require a bit of interop code to make it easily consumable in C#.

Optional parameters

We can define a C# function by writing the following piece of code:

```
public class CSharpExample {
    public static int Add(int x, int y = 1) {
        return x + y;
```

```
        }
    }
```

We can call the function in C# by writing the following piece of code:

```
var a = CSharpExample.Add(10)
var b = CSharpExample.Add(10, 20);
```

If we try the same with F#, it will work as well:

```
let a = CSharpExample.Add(10)
let b = CSharpExample.Add(10, 20)
```

Now, the other way around; a method defined in F# using the F# flavor of optional parameters is as follows:

```
type FSharp =
    static member Add(x, ?y) =
        let y = defaultArg y 1
        x + y
```

We can happily use it like this in F#:

```
let a = FSharp.Add(10)
let b = FSharp.Add(10, 20)
```

If we try to use this in C#, then we will see that it's not exposed as an optional parameter, so we will need to make the following changes:

```
type FSharp =
    static member Add(x, [<Optional;DefaultParameterValue(null)>]
?y) =
        let y = defaultArg y 1
        x + y
```

And then, in C#, we will use it as follows:

```
var a = FSharp.Add(10);
var b = FSharp.Add(10, FSharpOption<int>.Some(20));
```

As there is no syntactic sugar generation on the C# side, we will need to use the FSharpOption<'T> class directly.

Algebraic data types

F# discriminated unions are nothing but a bunch of classes generated by the F# compiler. Consider we have the following `Calculate` type:

```
type Calculate =
    | Add of int * int
    | Mult of int * int
```

In this case, we can use it directly in C# as follows:

```
var addObj = Calculate.NewAdd(10, 20)
var multObj = Calculate.NewMult(10, 20)
```

The only issue is deconstructing a discriminated union in C#; as C# doesn't have pattern matching, we can use the `is` operator to write the following piece of code:

```
if (addObj is Calculate.Add) {
    var addObjInstance = (Calculate.Add)addObj; }
```

Generic extensions consumable in C#

For a generic type, the type variable may not be constrained. You can now declare a C#-style extension member in F# to work around this limitation. When you combine this kind of declaration with the inline feature of F#, you can present generic algorithms as extension members:

```
[<Extension>]
type ExtraCSharpStyleExtensionMethodsInFSharp () =
    [<Extension>]
    static member inline Sum(xs: seq<'T>) = Seq.sum xs
let listOfIntegers = [ 1 .. 100 ]
let sum1 = listOfIntegers.Sum()
```

Exposing F# functionality to C#

We can follow a set of design principles to expose the functionality implemented in F# using unions, asynchronous workflows, or anything else:

- Wrap around the functionality with plain vanilla classes that just act as wrapper. This will make it easy to be consumed in any other .NET language, such as C#.
- Use .NET interfaces to expose functionality.

- Discriminated unions can have extension methods that can wrap around the functionality.

Summary

Although F# is considered a functional-first language, we have seen in this chapter that we can also talk of it as a multi-paradigm language. F# developers have, at their disposal, many of the tools frequently found in other more imperative languages, such as control flow structures (loops) and powerful OOP capabilities.

We have also seen how to use some of the most interesting features of C#, such as generics, LINQ queries, and events in F#. Finally, you learned how to make your F# program interop more easily with the C# code. In the next chapter, we will dive into the asynchronous features of F#.

5
Asynchronous Programming

Writing applications that are non-blocking or reacting to events is increasingly becoming important in this cloud world we live in. A modern application needs to carry out a rich user interaction, communicate with web services, react to notifications, and so on, which is why it is said that the execution of reactive applications is controlled by events. Asynchronous programming is characterized by many simultaneously pending reactions to internal or external events. These reactions may or may not be processed in parallel.

In .NET, both C#, and F# provide an asynchronous programming experience through keywords and syntaxes. In this chapter, we will go through the asynchronous programming model in F#, with a bit of cross-referencing or comparison drawn with the C# world.

In this chapter, we will cover the following topics:

- What the asynchronous workflows are and how to create them
- The main functions in the `FSharp.Core Async` module to manipulate `Async<'T>` types
- An introduction to the actor programming model using F# `MailboxProcessor`
- How to handle events in a reactive way

Asynchronous workflows in F#

Asynchronous (async) workflows are computation expressions that are set up to run asynchronously. It means that the system runs without blocking the current computation thread when an I/O or another asynchronous process is performed.

You may be wondering why do we need asynchronous programming, and why can't we just use the threading concepts that we have used for so long. The problem with OS threads is that the operation occupies the thread for the entire time that something happens, or when a computation is done. On the other hand, with asynchronous programming, the runtime will enable a thread only when it is required, otherwise it will be a normal code. There is also lot of marshalling and unmarshalling code (infrastructure code) that we will write around to overcome the issues that we face when directly dealing with the OS threads. Thus, async model allows the code to execute efficiently, still preventing locking the main thread when we perform expensive operations, like when we are performing an I/O operation over the network and there are a lot of incoming requests from the other endpoint.

There is a list of functions that the `Async` module in F# exposes to create or use these async workflows to program. The async pattern allows writing code that looks like it was written for a single-threaded program, but in the internals, it uses `async` blocks to execute. There are various triggering functions that provide a wide variety of ways to create the async workflow, which is either a background thread or a .NET framework `Task` object, or is running the computation in the current thread itself.

In this chapter, we will be using the example of downloading the content of a web page and modifying the data, as follows:

```
open System.IO
open System.Net

let downloadPage (url: string) =
    async {
        let req = HttpWebRequest.Create(url)
        use! resp = req.AsyncGetResponse()
        use respStream = resp.GetResponseStream()
        use sr = new StreamReader(respStream)
        return sr.ReadToEnd()
    }

downloadPage("https://www.google.com")
|> Async.RunSynchronously
```

The preceding function does the following:

1. The `async { ... }` expression generates an object of type `Async<string>`
2. These values are not actual results; rather, they are specifications of tasks that need to run and return a string
3. The `Async.RunSynchronously` method takes this object and runs it synchronously

We just wrote a simple function with async workflows with relative ease and reason about the code, which is much better than using code with `Begin/End` routines. One important point here is that the code is never blocked during the execution of the async workflow. This means that we can, in principle, have thousands of outstanding web requests, the limit being the number of concurrent threads supported by the machine.

Using let!

In async workflows, we will use the `let!` binding to enable execution to continue on other computations or threads while the computation is being performed. After the execution is complete, the rest of the async workflow is executed, thus simulating a sequential execution in an asynchronous way.

In addition to `let!`, we can also use `use!` to perform asynchronous bindings; basically, with `use!`, the object gets disposed when it loses the current scope.

In our previous example, we used `use!` to get the `HttpWebResponse` object; we can also do the following, the only difference being the response object will not be automatically disposed (by calling its `Dispose` method) when leaving scope.

```
let! resp = req.AsyncGetResponse()
// process response
```

We are using `let!` to start an operation and bind the result to a value; `do!` is used when the return of the `async` expression is a `unit`, as you can see in the following example:

```
do! Async.Sleep(1000)
```

Understanding async workflows

As explained earlier, async workflows are nothing but computation expressions with async patterns. In F#, we can define a computation expression with an expression builder, which is just a class whose methods should follow specific names and conventions. For example, the async builder implements the `Bind` and `Return` methods. This means that the `let!` expression is translated into a call to the `async.Bind` and `async.Return` function defined in the `Async` module in F# library. This is a compiler functionality to translate the `let!` expression into computation workflows, which remains transparent to the developer. The purpose of explaining this piece is to understand the internal workings of an async workflow, which is nothing but a computation expression.

The following listing shows the translated version of the `downloadPage` function we defined earlier:

```
async.Delay(fun() ->
    let req = HttpWebRequest.Create(url)
    async.Bind(req.AsyncGetResponse(), fun resp ->
        async.Using(resp, fun resp ->
            let respStream = resp.GetResponseStream()
            async.Using(new StreamReader(respStream), fun sr ->
                reader.ReadToEnd()
            )
        )
    )
)
```

The following things are happening in the workflow:

1. The `Delay` function wraps the code in a lambda to defer execution.
2. The body of the lambda creates an `HttpWebRequest` call, which is bound to the `req` variable.
3. The `AsyncGetResponse` method is called, and another lambda is generated, which will be invoked when the operation is completed.

   The `AsyncGetResponse` is a method extension present in the F# core `Async` module.

4. The `Using` function then creates a closure to dispose the object, which must implement the `IDisposable` interface, once the workflow is complete.

Async module

We saw how to create async workflows. Now, we will see the `Async` module, which contains a list of functions that allows writing or consuming asynchronous code. We will go through each function in detail, with an example, to understand it better.

Async.AsBeginEnd

It is very useful to expose the F# workflow functionality out of F#, say if we want to consume the API in C#. The `Async.AsBeginEnd` function gives the possibility of exposing the async workflows as a tuple of three methods (`Begin`/`End`/`Cancel`) following the original .NET asynchronous programming model.

Based on our `downloadPage` function, we can define the `Begin`, `End`, and `Cancel` functions as follows. This way, it will be possible from C# to instantiate the `Downloader` type and use it without async workflows.

```
type Downloader() =
    let beginMethod, endMethod, cancelMethod =
        Async.AsBeginEnd downloadPage
    member this.BeginDownload(url, callback, state : obj) =
        beginMethod(url, callback, state)
    member this.EndDownload(ar) =
        endMethod ar
    member this.CancelDownload(ar) =
        cancelMethod(ar)
```

> Since the release of .NET 4.5 and C# 5.0, C# programs tend to use more `Task`, which is compatible with the `async`/`await` keywords, than this pattern to handle async programming.

Async.AwaitEvent

The `Async.AwaitEvent` function creates an async computation that waits for a single invocation of a .NET framework event by adding a handler to the event, as shown in the following code block:

```
type MyEvent(v : string) =
    inherit EventArgs()
    member this.Value = v;
let testAwaitEvent (evt : IEvent<MyEvent>) = async {
    printfn "Before waiting"
    let! r = Async.AwaitEvent evt
    printfn "After waiting: %O" r.Value
    do! Async.Sleep(1000)
    return ()
    }

let runAwaitEventTest () =
    let evt = new Event<Handler<MyEvent>, _>()
    Async.Start <| testAwaitEvent evt.Publish
    System.Threading.Thread.Sleep(3000)
    printfn "Before raising"
    evt.Trigger(null, new MyEvent("value"))
    printfn "After raising"
```

The preceding program outputs as following:

```
> runAwaitEventTest();;
> Before waiting
> Before raising
> After raising
> After waiting : value
```

The `testAwaitEvent` function listens to the event using `Async.AwaitEvent` and prints the value. As `Async.Start` will take some time to start up the thread, we will simply call `Thread.Sleep` to wait on the main thread. This is for example purposes only. We can think of scenarios where a button click event is awaited and used inside an `async` block.

Async.AwaitIAsyncResult

The `Async.AwaitIAsyncResult` function creates a computation result and waits for the `IAsyncResult` interface to complete. The `IAsyncResult` interface is the async programming model interface common to other .NET languages that allows you to write async programs. It returns `true` if `IAsyncResult` issues a signal within a given timeout. The timeout parameter is optional and its default value is -1 equivalent to `Timeout.Infinite`, as shown in the following example:

```
let testAwaitIAsyncResult (url: string) =
    async {
        let req = HttpWebRequest.Create(url)
        let aResp = req.BeginGetResponse(null, null)
        let! asyncResp = Async.AwaitIAsyncResult(aResp, 1000)
        if asyncResp then
            let resp = req.EndGetResponse(aResp)
            use respStream = resp.GetResponseStream()
            use sr = new StreamReader(respStream)
            return sr.ReadToEnd()
        else return ""
    }
> Async.RunSynchronously (testAwaitIAsyncResult
"https://www.google.com")
```

We will modify the `downloadPage` example with `AwaitIAsyncResult`; this allows a bit more flexibility when we want to add timeouts as well. In the preceding example, the `AwaitIAsyncResult` method handle will wait for `1000` milliseconds and then execute the next steps.

Async.AwaitWaitHandle

The `Async.AwaitWaitHandle` function creates a computation that waits on a wait handle. Wait handles are a mechanism to coordinate work between threads. The following is an example with `ManualResetEvent`:

```
let testAwaitWaitHandle waitHandle = async {
    printfn "Before waiting"
    let! r = Async.AwaitWaitHandle waitHandle
    printfn "After waiting"
}
let runTestAwaitWaitHandle () =
    let event = new System.Threading.ManualResetEvent(false)
    Async.Start <| testAwaitWaitHandle event
    System.Threading.Thread.Sleep(3000)
    printfn "Before raising"
    event.Set() |> ignore
    printfn "After raising"
```

The example uses `ManualResetEvent` to show how to use `AwaitHandle`, which is very similar to the event example we saw in the previous topic.

Async.AwaitTask

The `Async.AwaitTask` function returns an async computation that waits for the given task to complete and returns its result. This helps in consuming C# APIs that expose task-based async operations:

```
let downloadPageAsTask (url: string) =
    async {
        let req = HttpWebRequest.Create(url)
        use! resp = req.AsyncGetResponse()
        use respStream = resp.GetResponseStream()
        use sr = new StreamReader(respStream)
        return sr.ReadToEnd()
    }
    |> Async.StartAsTask

let testAwaitTask (t: Task<string>) =
    async {
        let! r = Async.AwaitTask t
        return r
    }
> downloadPageAsTask "https://www.google.com"
  |> testAwaitTask
  |> Async.RunSynchronously;;
```

The preceding function is also downloading the web page as HTML content, but it starts the operation as a .NET `Task` object.

Async.FromBeginEnd

The `FromBeginEnd` function acts as an adapter for an API using the original .NET asynchronous model by wrapping the provided `Begin`/`End` methods. Thus, it allows using a large number of existing components that support the `IAsyncResult` interface. We will look at the same download page example using `FromBeginEnd`, as follows:

```
let downloadPageBeginEnd (url: string) =
    async {
        let req = HttpWebRequest.Create(url)
        use! resp = Async.FromBeginEnd(req.BeginGetResponse,
req.EndGetResponse)
        use respStream = resp.GetResponseStream()
        use sr = new StreamReader(respStream)
        return sr.ReadToEnd()
    }
```

The function accepts two parameters and automatically identifies the return type; we will use `BeginGetResponse` and `EndGetResponse` as our functions to call. Internally, `Async.FromBeginEnd` delegates the asynchronous operation and gets back the handle once the `EndGetResponse` function is called.

Async.FromContinuations

The `Async.FromContinuations` function creates an async computation that captures the current success, exception, and cancellation continuations. This is very useful when we want to transform code using callbacks to an async workflow. To understand these three operations, let's create a `sleep` function similar to `Async.Sleep` using `timer`:

```
open System.Threading

let sleep t = Async.FromContinuations(fun (cont, erFun, _) ->
    let rec timer = new Timer(TimerCallback(callback))
    and callback state =
        timer.Dispose()
        cont(())
    timer.Change(t, Timeout.Infinite) |> ignore
    )

let testSleep = async {
```

```
            printfn "Before"
            do! sleep 5000
            printfn "After 5000 msecs"
            }
    Async.RunSynchronously testSleep
```

The `sleep` function takes an integer and returns a `unit`; it uses
`Async.FromContinuations` to allow the flow of the program to continue when a `timer`
event is raised. It does so by calling the `cont(())` function, which is a continuation to allow
the next step in the async flow to execute. If there is any error, we can call `erFun` to throw
the exception and it will be handled from the place where we are calling this function.

Using the `FromContinuation` function helps us wrap and expose functionality that can be
used inside async workflows. It also helps you control the execution of the program by
canceling or throwing errors using simple APIs.

Async.Start

The `Async.Start` function starts the async computation in the thread pool. It accepts an
`Async<unit>` function to start the async computation. The `downloadPage` function can be
started as follows:

```
let asyncDownloadPage(url) = async {
        let! result = downloadPage(url)
        printfn "%s" result }
asyncDownloadPage "http://www.google.com"
|> Async.Start
```

We wrap the function to another async function that returns an `Async<unit>` so it can be
called by `Async.Start`.

Async.StartChild

The `Async.StartChild` function starts a child computation within an async workflow.
This allows multiple async computations to be executed simultaneously, as shown in the
following piece of code:

```
let subTask v = async    {
        printfn "Task %d started" v
        Thread.Sleep (v * 1000)
        printfn "Task %d finished" v
        return v
        }
```

```
let mainTask = async    {
    printfn "Main task started"
    let! childTask1 = Async.StartChild (subTask 1)
    let! childTask2 = Async.StartChild (subTask 5)
    printfn "Subtasks started"
    let! child1Result = childTask1
    printfn "Subtask1 result: %d" child1Result
    let! child2Result = childTask2
    printfn "Subtask2 result: %d" child2Result
    printfn "Subtasks completed"
    return ()
}
Async.RunSynchronously mainTask
```

As you may have noticed, when `Async.StartChild` is used, the code keeps executing and does not wait for the task to finish (`childTask` is still an `Async` value). It is not until we await the task directly (`let! child1Result = childTask1`) that the workflow stops executing to await the result of the operation. This is useful when we want to start several tasks in parallel but then we want to get the results in a specific order.

Async.StartAsTask

The `Async.StartAsTask` function executes a computation in the thread pool and returns a `Task` object that will be completed in the corresponding state once the computation terminates. We can use the same example of starting the `downloadPage` function as a `Task` object, as shown in the following code block:

```
let downloadPageAsTask (url: string) =
    async {
        let req = HttpWebRequest.Create(url)
        use! resp = req.AsyncGetResponse()
        use respStream = resp.GetResponseStream()
        use sr = new StreamReader(respStream)
        return sr.ReadToEnd()
    }
    |> Async.StartAsTask
let task = downloadPageAsTask("http://www.google.com")
printfn "Do some work"
task.Wait()
printfn "done"
```

Unlike C#, F# programs tend to use more `async` than `Task`. Both types are similar, but there are semantic differences (for example, tasks start immediately after their creation while F# `async` must be explicitly awaited), and also historical reasons as `async` was already present in F# before `Task` appeared in C#.

Async.StartChildAsTask

The `Async.StartChildAsTask` function creates an async computation from within an async computation that starts the following computation as a `Task`.

```
let testAwaitTask = async {
    printfn "Starting"
    let! child = Async.StartChildAsTask <| async {   //
    Async.StartChildAsTask shall be described later
            printfn "Child started"
            Thread.Sleep(5000)
            printfn "Child finished"
            return 100
        }
    printfn "Waiting for the child task"
    let! result = Async.AwaitTask child
    print "Child result %d" result
    }
```

Async.StartImmediate

The `Async.StartImmediate` function runs an async computation that, unlike when `Async.Start` is used, is guaranteed to finish in the same thread. This is very important when we start async operations in the GUI thread because, usually, we will need to manipulate a GUI element with the result (for example, to display it in a textbox) and this causes an error if it is done from a different thread.

```
let asyncDownloadPage(url) = async {
    let! result = downloadPage(url)
    printfn "%s" result }
asyncDownloadPage "http://www.google.com"
|> Async.StartImmediate
```

Async.SwitchToNewThread

The `Async.SwitchToNewThread` function creates an async computation that creates a new thread and runs its continuation in that thread:

```
let asyncDownloadPage(url) = async {
    do! Async.SwitchToNewThread()
    let! result = downloadPage(url)
    printfn "%s" result }
asyncDownloadPage "http://www.google.com"
|> Async.Start
```

Async.SwitchToThreadPool

The `Async.SwitchToThreadPool` function creates an async computation that queues a work item which runs its continuation, as shown in the following piece of code:

```
let asyncDownloadPage(url) = async {
    do! Async.SwitchToNewThread()
    let! result = downloadPage(url)
    do! Async.SwitchToThreadPool()
    printfn "%s" result }
asyncDownloadPage "http://www.google.com"
|> Async.Start
```

Async.SwitchToContext

The `Async.SwitchToContext` function creates an async computation that runs its continuation in the `Post` method of the synchronization context. Let's assume that we set the text from the `downloadPage` function to a UI textbox, then we would do it as follows:

```
let syncContext = System.Threading.SynchronizationContext()
let asyncDownloadPage(url) = async {
    do! Async.SwitchToContext(syncContext)
    let! result = downloadPage(url)
    textbox.Text <- result }
asyncDownloadPage "http://www.google.com"
|> Async.Start
```

In console applications, the context will be null.

Async.Parallel

The `Parallel` function allows you to execute individual async computations in parallel by queueing them in the thread pool, as follows:

```
let parallel_download() =
    let sites = ["http://www.bing.com";
                 "http://www.google.com";
                 "http://www.yahoo.com";
                 "http://www.search.com"]
    let htmlOfSites =
        Async.Parallel [for site in sites -> downloadPage site ]
        |> Async.RunSynchronously
    printfn "%A" htmlOfSites
```

We can use the same example of downloading HTML content in a parallel way. The preceding example shows the essence of parallel I/O computation as follows:

- The `async { .... }` expression in the `downloadPage` function shows the async computation
- These are then composed in parallel using a `fork/join` combinator under the hood
- In this sample, the composition is synchronously awaited for the overall result

Async.OnCancel

The `Async.OnCancel` function generates a disposable handler that triggers an operation if the async workflow is canceled before the handler is disposed, as shown in the following example:

```
let simulatedLengthyOperation() =
    async {
        // Async.Sleep checks for cancellation at the end of the
interval,
        // loop over many short intervals instead of sleeping for a
long one.
                while true do
                do! Async.Sleep(100)
    }

    let computation id
    (tokenSource:System.Threading.CancellationTokenSource) =
        async {
            use! cancelHandler = Async.OnCancel(fun () ->
                printfn "Lengthy operation %s cancelled" id)
```

```
                        do! simulatedLengthyOperation()
        }
        |> fun workflow -> Async.Start(workflow, tokenSource.Token)

    let tokenSource1 = new System.Threading.CancellationTokenSource()
    let tokenSource2 = new System.Threading.CancellationTokenSource()

    computation "A" tokenSource1
    computation "B" tokenSource2
    printfn "Started computations."
    System.Threading.Thread.Sleep(1000)
    printfn "Sending cancellation signal."
    tokenSource2.Cancel()
    tokenSource1.Cancel()
```

Actor programming with MailboxProcessor

The actor programming model is a concurrent programming technique that provides a powerful mechanism to encapsulate several concurrency features. The key principles of the actor model are as follows:

- No shared state between actors
- Async message passing between clients to actor or between actors
- Mailbox to buffer incoming messages
- React to received messages by executing function

The F# MailboxProcessor class is the implementation of the actor model in FSharp.Core, and it is essentially a dedicated message queue running its own thread. We can use the API for MailboxProcessor to Post/Receive messages synchronously or asynchronously. We can also consider it an agent with an internal state machine. Let's take look at our first async agent:

```
let agent =
   MailboxProcessor.Start(fun inbox ->
     async { while true do
                let! msg = inbox.Receive()
                printfn "got message '%s'" msg } )
> agent.Post "Hello World"
> got message 'Hello World'
```

The agent performs repeated async waits for messages and prints each message it receives. In the preceding agent, we see two important things, as follows:

- `Start`: This defines the async callback that forms the message looping
- `Receive`: This is the async function to receive messages from the internal queue

One of the keys to successful agent programming in F# is isolation. Isolation means that resources exist which belong to a specific agent, and are not accessed, except by that agent. This means the isolated state is protected from concurrent access and data races.

We can also use agents to write thread-safe programs as isolation is guaranteed. The internal dictionary is private to the async agent, and no capability to read or write to the dictionary is made available outside of the agent. This means that the mutable state in the dictionary is isolated. Non-concurrent, safe access is guaranteed:

```
open System.Collections.Generic

let dictAgent =
    MailboxProcessor.Start(fun inbox ->
        async { let strings = Dictionary<string,int>()
                while true do
                let! msg = inbox.Receive()
                if strings.ContainsKey msg then
                    strings.[msg] <- strings.[msg] + 1
                else
                    strings.[msg] <- 0
                printfn "message '%s' now seen '%d' times" msg
strings.[msg] } )

[ "Hello"; "World"; "Hello"; "John"; ]
|> List.iter (dictAgent.Post)
message 'Hello' now seen '0' times
message 'World' now seen '0' times
message 'Hello' now seen '1' times
message 'John' now seen '0' times
```

Design patterns with MailboxProcessor

We can follow these generic design patterns to use mailboxes in F#:

- Imperative definition using `while` loops
- Functional definition using recursive loops

As mailboxes process one message at a time, it can also hold an internal state of its own; we have already seen we can make an internal state thread-safe.

Type-safe MailboxProcessor, an imperative approach

We can use `while` loops to define our `async` block as follows:

```
let agent =
    MailboxProcessor.Start(fun inbox ->
        async {
            // isolated imperative state goes here
            ...
            while <condition> do
                // read messages and respond
                let! msg = inbox.Receive()
                ...
    })
```

With `while` loops, we will need to maintain a mutable internal state that can be updated based on the message that is being processed. Let's assume that we are doing a `Begin/End` transaction workflow with a mailbox, which we will write it as follows:

```
type Transaction =
    | Begin
    | End

type TransactionState =
    {
        mutable isInTransaction : bool
    }
let transactionAgent =
    Agent<Transaction>.Start(fun inbox ->
        async {
            let tState : TransactionState  = { isInTransaction = false }
            while true do
                let! msg = inbox.Receive()
                match msg with
                | Begin ->
                    tState.isInTransaction <- true
                    printfn "begin transaction"
                | End ->
                    tState.isInTransaction <- false
                    printfn "end transaction"
    })
> transactionAgent.Post(Begin);;
begin transaction
```

```
> transactionAgent.Post(End);;
end transaction
```

In the preceding example, the transaction agent handles two messages–Begin and End–and on receiving the message, it updates a mutable isInTransaction property as true/false. As we can see, we must resort to using mutable representation of the state object, even though it is thread-safe and accessed only once during the entire loop.

Type-safe MailboxProcessor, a functional approach

In functional definitions, we can use a recursive loop to define our loop with an internal state, and this gives an easy way to define immutable state. Consider the following example:

```
type Transaction =
    | Begin
    | End

type TransactionState =
    {
        isInTransaction : bool
    }
let transactionAgent =
    MailboxProcessor<Transaction>.Start(fun inbox ->
            let rec loop (state: TransactionState) = async {
                let! msg = inbox.Receive()
                match msg with
                | Begin ->
                    printfn "begin transaction"
                    return! loop { state with isInTransaction = true }
                | End ->
                    printfn "end transaction"
                    return! loop { state with isInTransaction = false }
            }
            loop ({ isInTransaction = false })
        )
> transactionAgent.Post(Begin);;
begin transaction
> transactionAgent.Post(End);;
end transaction
```

The async block in the functional definition has a recursive loop that maintains an internal state within the loop; because of this, it is important to take the tail-call optimization into account, as we saw in Chapter 1, *Getting Started in F#*.

Messages and union types

It is common to use a discriminated union for a message type. For example, for an agent-based calculator, we will define the union type as follows:

```
type Calculator =
    | Add of int * int
    | Multiply of int * int

let calculatorAgent =
    MailboxProcessor<Calculator>.Start(fun inbox ->
        let rec loop() = async {
            let! msg = inbox.Receive()
            match msg with
            | Add(x, y) ->
                printfn "Add - %d" (x + y)
                return! loop()

            | Multiply(x, y) ->
                printfn "Multi - %d" (x * y)
                return! loop()
        }

        loop()
    )
> calculatorAgent.Post(Add(10, 20));;
Add - 30
```

Using `type.safe` messages like this is a good idea in many circumstances. Furthermore, union types allow us to use pattern matching when checking the message. However, when we look at distributed computing, then we may have to serialize the data in binary or encoded string so that messages can be consumed by other actors who can process the type of the message. This is usually not an issue with `MailboxProcessor` as it runs only in a single process of a local machine, but it will be important when using other actor systems that can spawn agents through several machines in a network such as **Akka.NET**, as we will see in `Chapter 10`, *Distributed Programming with F#*.

Reporting results from the mailbox

Many times, once we process a message, we may have to reply back to the requestor or the originator. The `MailboxProcessor` class provides some APIs through which we can reply back, and it also wraps the function definition as an async or synchronous call. Let's look at its definition with the following example:

```
type CalculatorMsg =
```

```
      | Add of int * int * AsyncReplyChannel<int>
      | Multiply of int * int * AsyncReplyChannel<int>
  type CalculatorAgent () =
      let agent =
          MailboxProcessor<CalculatorMsg>.Start(fun inbox ->
              let rec loop() = async {
                  let! msg = inbox.Receive()
                  match msg with
                  | Add(x, y, r) ->
                      let result = x + y
                      r.Reply(result)
                      return! loop()

                  | Multiply(x, y, r) ->
                      let result = x * y
                      r.Reply(result)
                      return! loop()
              }

              loop()
          )

      member this.Add(x: int, y: int): int =
          agent.PostAndReply(fun r -> CalculatorMsg.Add(x, y, r))

      member this.AddAsync(x: int, y: int): Async<int> =
          agent.PostAndAsyncReply(fun r -> CalculatorMsg.Add(x, y, r))

      member this.Multiply(x: int, y: int): int =
          agent.PostAndReply(fun r -> CalculatorMsg.Multiply(x, y, r))

      member this.MultiplyAsync(x: int, y: int): Async: int =
          agent.PostAndAsyncReply(fun r -> CalculatorMsg.Multiply(x, y,
r))
```

We will define a class that exposes functions of `Add` and `Multiply`, both synchronous and async definitions. We will use the agent as an internal state machine that does all the business logic and exposes to the outside world with simple .NET APIs. This is also very helpful in writing consumable APIs for other .NET languages.

The important point to note is the `AsyncReplyChannel` class definition in the `CalculatorMsg` union type. This defines a reply channel parameter that we will pass along with the other parameters to the mailbox. And once the computation is complete, we can use the `Reply` function to return the results from the mailbox. The function `PostAndReply` or `PostAndAsyncReply` has a function callback with the reply channel object.

We will simply need to pass it along with the following message:

```
agent.PostAndReply(fun r -> CalculatorMsg.Add(x, y, r))
```

 Note that you should always keep the reply channel as the last parameter in your union type definition.

To use this calculator agent, we will simply create an object and use the APIs that are exposed to us:

```
> let c = new CalculatorAgent();;
> c.Add(10, 20);;
val it : int = 30
```

Likewise, if we are inside an `async` block, then we can call the async functions to evaluate the results.

Agents and errors

Good error detection, reporting, and logging are essential in actor programming. Let's take a look at how to detect and forward errors when using F# mailbox processors.

F# async workflows catch exceptions and propagate them automatically within `async {  ... }` blocks, even across async waits and I/O operations. You can also use `try/with`, `try/finally`, and use constructs within the `async {  ... }` blocks to catch exceptions and release resources. This means that we will only need to deal with uncaught errors in agents. When an errors is uncaught in the `MailboxProcessor` class, the `Error` event on the agent is raised. A common pattern is to forward all errors to a supervising actor, as shown in the following code block:

```
let error_supervisor =
    MailboxProcessor<System.Exception>.Start(fun inbox ->
        async { while true do
                    let! err = inbox.Receive()
                    printfn "an error '%A' occurred in an agent" err })
let agent =
    new MailboxProcessor<int>(fun inbox ->
        async { while true do
                    let! msg = inbox.Receive()
                    if msg % 100 = 0 then
                        failwith "I don't like that cookie!" })
agent.Error.Add(fun error -> error_supervisor.Post error)
agent.Start()
```

The preceding example reports an error when we have received `100` messages. When executing the following error agent, `MailboxProcessor` does not have more supervision capabilities built in:

```
an error 'I don't like that cookie!' occurred in an agent
```

If we want more advanced functionality, for example, making the supervisor restart the failing actor, we will need to implement it ourselves. In `Chapter 10`, *Distributed Programming with F#*, we will see how supervision is a central concept in another actor system implementation, Akka.NET.

MailboxProcessor functions

The `MailboxProcessor` class provides easy-to-use APIs. The following is the list of functions:

Signature	Description

`Receive: ?int -> Async<'Msg>`
 	
`TryReceive: ?int ->`
`Async<'Msg option>`
	This waits for a message and consumes the first message in the arrival order. It uses a queue internally:
	`let agent =`
	    `MailboxProcessor.Start(fun    inbox ->`
	      `async { while true do`
	            `let! msg =`
	`inbox.Receive()`
	            `printfn "got    message`
	`'%s'"`
	            `msg } )`

`Post: 'Msg -> unit`	This posts a message to the queue asynchronously: `agent.Post "Hello World"`

`PostAndAsyncReply:`
`(AsyncReplyChannel<'Reply>`
`-> 'Msg) * ?int ->`
`Async<'Reply>`
	This posts a message to an agent and awaits a reply on the channel asynchronously:
	
	``
	type Action =
	
		MessageAndReply of int *
		AsyncReplyChannel<int>
		let replyChannelAgent =
		        MailboxProcessor<Action>.Start(fun
		        inbox ->
		          async {
		                let! msg = inbox.Receive()
		                match msg with
		
			MessageAndReply(v,
			channel)
			                      ->
			                      channel.Reply(v)
			              }
			          )
			    let postAndAsyncReply() =
			    replyChannelAgent.PostAndAsyncReply(fun r
			->
			    Action.MessageAndReply(10, r))
			``

`PostAndReply:`
`(AsyncReplyChannel<'Reply>`
`-> 'Msg) * ?int -> 'Reply`
 	
`TryPostAndReply:`
`(AsyncReplyChannel<'Reply>`
`-> 'Msg) * ?int ->`
`Async<'Reply option>`
	This posts a message to an agent and awaits a reply on the channel synchronously:
	
	``
	let postAndReply() =
	            replyChannelAgent.PostAndReply(fun
	r
	    -> Action.MessageAndReply(10, r))
	``

`PostAndTryAsyncReply:`
`(AsyncReplyChannel<'Reply>`
`-> 'Msg) * ?int ->`
`Async<'Reply option>`
	This is similar to `PostAndAsyncReply`, but returns None within the timeout:
	
	``
	let postAndTryAsyncReply() =
	replyChannelAgent.PostAndTryAsyncReply((fun
	    r -> Action.MessageAndReply(10, r)),
	100)
	``
	Timeout functions are useful when we are trying to query from a database or web service.

`Scan: ('Msg -> Async<'T>` `option) * ?int -> Async<'T>` `TryScan: ('Msg -> Async<'T>` `option) * ?int -> Async<'T` `option>`	This scans for a message by looking through messages in arrival order until a provided function returns a Some value. Other messages remain in the queue. The standard use of Scan is with cooperative agents: ```let loop () = async {` ` let! res = mbox.TryScan(function` `	ImportantMessage -> Some(async {` ` // process message` ` return 0` ` })` `	_ -> None)` ` match res with` `	None ->` ` // perform some check & continue` `waiting` ` return! loop ()` `	Some n ->` ` // ImportantMessage was received` ` and processed` `}```` In the preceding example, there is a union type with ImportantMessage that is being scanned and executed, and the rest is executed in a different workflow loop. This kind of pattern is very useful in modularizing the message loops.
`Start:` `(MailboxProcessor<'Msg> ->` `Async<unit>) *` `?CancellationToken ->` `MailboxProcessor<'Msg>`	This creates and starts an agent: ```let simpleAgent =` ` new MailboxProcessor<_>(fun inbox` `->` ` async { while true do` ` let! msg =` `inbox.Receive()` ` printfn "got message` `'%s'"` ` msg` ` })` `simpleAgent.Start()` `simpleAgent.Post "Hello World"```

Implementing a non-blocking queue

A non-blocking queue is a queue that will enqueue/dequeue in a thread-safe manner. If there are multiple threads trying to access the same queue, it will still return in the sequence in which the items were added. We can first start with declaring the different types of messages that the NonBlockingQueue class will require:

```
open System.Collections.Generic
open System.Threading

type internal Action<'T> =
    | Put of 'T * AsyncReplyChannel<unit>
    | Get of AsyncReplyChannel<'T>
    | Count of AsyncReplyChannel<int>
```

Each message implements a functionality that we want to achieve in the queue, which are as follows:

- Put: This has an input generic parameter 'T and a reply channel with unit. The reason to use a unit here is to notify the user that the function has returned after adding to the queue. If we don't use a reply channel, then the caller function will immediately return and the user may be expecting the order in which the items were enqueued, and while being dequeued it was not the same.
- Get: This has a reply channel so we can use it to return the first element of the queue.
- Count: These return back the current count in the queue.

We will now declare the NonBlockingQueue<'T> class; we want to keep it generic, so we can use any type within the blocking queue. The type implements the following:

- The mbox agent that implements the earlier given messages. It has an internal state with a standard .NET queue object. The loop is a recursive one, and we can follow the functional definition pattern to implement this mailbox.
- There is a CancellationTokenSource object that is passed to the mailbox, so when we dispose the blocking queue, the internal async thread is also disposed.
- The messages are implemented inside the recursive loop, and we keep returning the loop so we can create an async continuation. The continuation helps the code to keep running in an async way.
- The internals of the message reception and implementation simply uses the standard .NET queue functionalities of Enqueue, Dequeue, and Count, although we can also have an array and implement our own queue as well here.

- We can also implement an `IDisposable` interface to cancel the async thread:

```
type NonBlockingQueue<'T>() =
    let cts = new CancellationTokenSource()

    let mbox = MailboxProcessor<Action<'T>>.Start(fun inbox ->
                  let rec loop(queue: Queue<'T>) = async {
                      let! msg = inbox.Receive()
                      match msg with
                      | Put(v, r) ->
                          queue.Enqueue(v)
                          r.Reply(())
                          return! loop queue

                      | Get(r) ->
                          queue.Dequeue()
                          |> r.Reply
                          return! loop queue

                      | Count(r) ->
                          queue.Count
                          |> r.Reply
                          return! loop queue
                  }

                  loop (new Queue<'T>())
               , cts.Token)
```

We can now wrap the mailbox implementation with simple easy-to-use functions, as shown in the following code block:

```
member x.Enqueue(v) =
    mbox.PostAndReply(fun r -> Action.Put(v,r))

member x.EnqueueAsync(v) =
    mbox.PostAndAsyncReply(fun r -> Action.Put(v, r))

member x.Dequeue() =
    mbox.PostAndReply(fun r -> Action.Get(r))

member x.DequeueAsync() =
    mbox.PostAndAsyncReply(fun r -> Action.Get(r))

member x.Count = mbox.PostAndReply(Action.Count)

interface System.IDisposable with
    member x.Dispose() =
```

```
                    cts.Cancel()
```

Let's use the queue and try to access it from different threads. We will first need to set up an environment in which there are multiple threads trying to access this queue:

```
    let bQueue = new NonBlockingQueue<string>()
        let r = new System.Random()

        let generate() =
            let rec loop(i) = async {
                if i < 10 then
                    bQueue.Enqueue(r.NextDouble() |> string)
                    printfn "Thread Id : %d"
  Thread.CurrentThread.ManagedThreadId
                    return! loop(i+1)
            }

            loop(0)

        generate() |> Async.Start
        generate() |> Async.Start
```

The preceding example run simply creates an async thread and pushes values into a global bQueue object. When we run this in the interactive window, we will get the following output:

```
>
Thread Id : Thread Id : 10
11
Thread Id : 11
Thread Id : 11
Thread Id : 11
Thread Id : 11
Thread Id : 10
Thread Id : 10
Thread Id : 10
Thread Id : 10
Thread Id : 10
Thread Id : 10
Thread Id : 10
Thread Id : 10
Thread Id : 11
Thread Id : 11
Thread Id : 11
Thread Id : 11
Thread Id : 11
```

```
> bQueue.Count;;
val it : int = 20
```

The items are enqueued in the queue in a thread-safe manner, so no two threads are accessing the same object at any given time, thus avoiding situations such as deadlocks. Likewise, we can also use the `Dequeue` function to query the `NonBlockingQueue` class in a thread-safe manner.

Using `MailboxProcessor` helps you write thread-safe code in order to fulfill any requirement using the simple design patterns we have discussed up until now.

Reactive programming with async workflows

We will now generalize the `async` model so that it can be used not only in async workflows, but also with `IObservable` streams to achieve reactiveness. The `IObservable` interface is used to manipulate events as if they were sequences (or streams). The main difference with `IEnumerable` is that the latter is pull-based (our code decides when to pull the next item from the sequence) while the former is push-based; we do not know when the next event will happen so we can only react to new inputs in the stream.

 The `FSharp.Core` library also provides functions in the `Event` module to manipulate events directly, as if they were streams, without having to convert them to `IObservable`.

This means that we need constructs that can create observables, as opposed to only async workflows. Essentially, it should be possible to await all kinds of events produced by `Event` or `IObservable` streams. In this section, we will only go through the default options available in the `FSharp.Core` library, and not with the **Reactive Extensions** (**Rx**), which is a very popular open source library providing many more functions to manipulate `IObservable` streams.

F# doesn't provide `Async.AwaitObservable` in the core library, so we will focus on event streams using `Async.AwaitEvent`. The `Event` module has an `Event.merge` function that can merge two events as one output from the F# source code if we look up the source code to `Event.map`, `Event.merge`, and `Choice`:

```
type Choice<'T1,'T2> =
    | Choice1Of2 of 'T1
    | Choice2Of2 of 'T2

let map f (w: IEvent<'Delegate,'T>) =
```

```
let ev = new Event<_>()
w.Add(fun x -> ev.Trigger(f x));
ev.Publish

let merge (w1: IEvent<'Del1,'T>) (w2: IEvent<'Del2,'T>) =
    let ev = new Event<_>()
    w1.Add(fun x -> ev.Trigger(x));
    w2.Add(fun x -> ev.Trigger(x));
    ev.Publish
```

We can simplify our event streaming by unifying them as follows:

```
open System.Drawing
open System.Windows.Forms

type UserEvents =
| Dragging of MouseEventArgs
| KeyPress of KeyEventArgs

    with
        static member CreateEvent (e1: IEvent<MouseEventArgs>, e2:
        IEvent<MouseEventArgs>) =
            let ev = new Event<_>()
            e1.Add(fun x -> ev.Trigger(Dragging x))
            e2.Add(fun x -> ev.Trigger(Dragging x))
            ev.Publish

        static member CreateEvent (e1: IEvent<KeyEventArgs>, e2:
        IEvent<KeyEventArgs>) =
            let ev = new Event<_>()
            e1.Add(fun x -> ev.Trigger(KeyPress x))
            e2.Add(fun x -> ev.Trigger(KeyPress x))
            ev.Publish
```

Additionally, we can write this code inside an async workflow, as follows:

```
async {
let dragging = UserEvents.CreateEvent form.MouseDown form.MouseUp
let! move = Async.AwaitEvent dragging
// further code }
```

So, as we see, this gives a more generic approach to merging different streams and using the async patterns to utilize reactive streams.

We can also use `Choice` union types to define generic choices in the output of these streams, so we can just do a simple `let!` and `match` combination to process the results. It will be a simpler version of the mailbox processor pattern:

```
async {
    let merged = Event.merge
                        (form.KeyDown |> Event.map Choice1Of2)
                        (form.MouseMove |> Event.map Choice2Of2)
    let! evt = Async.AwaitEvent merged
    match evt with     | Choice1Of2(x)  ->
    // further code
}
```

 Note that it is assuming we have an object that is a `Windows.Forms` object.

Here, it is easier to merge many different event types into a unified union of the type `Choice`.

As we can see, F# can allow both the consuming and creating of observable streams in a direct style, avoiding low-level callbacks in many cases, within the async workflow. And, it looks like a seemingly fitting model with the async workflows that we saw in the earlier sections.

Summary

In this chapter, we went through, in detail, explanations of the different semantics in async programming with F#, the mailbox processor, and the different design patterns, then finally performed some reactive programming streams and used them with async workflows.

In the next chapter, we will look at type providers in F# and how to create a custom type provider to implement your own metadata system.

6

Type Providers

Type providers are part of the F# 3.0 language features that support information-rich programming. With so much diverse information available over the Internet and different data modeling systems, it is always a pain to write parsers or manually decode the data to some form that we understand. Adding to that the transformations which happen at runtime, meaning that any changes in the data model will raise exceptions, altogether represent a nightmare for developers to maintain their projects. The .NET framework has ways to deal with this by creating code using generators, but there are risks involved when the underlying data model changes–the developer has to regenerate the code and deploy it again.

In addition to the F# scripting system, type providers help interactive development by exposing the metadata of the underlying model as a strongly typed .NET class. This is a very easy way to do an exploratory analysis of the underlying data. As the type providers generate types on the fly, it can provide different signatures depending on the settings the type provider is initialized to. For example, the SQL type provider can generate different models based on the connection string to different databases. This allows for a very direct approach, and also an on-demand integration of large-scale information datasets available online in a strongly typed manner, for example, Wikipedia.

When necessary, we can also create our own custom type providers using the helper libraries that are available in the F# API for type providers. This would be the case when we don't find a type provider for a specific dataset; we can then build our own to read the schema and present the data available to the programmer in a strongly typed way. In any case, there are many type providers that also work with languages such as schema and provide a strongly typed access via F#, for example, R, the language used by statisticians in research, has a type provider that can query the R system and get back results in a strongly typed way.

In this chapter, we will cover the following topics:

- Type providers:
    - SQL type provider
    - **OData** type provider
    - Web service type provider
- Data analysis using type providers
- Query builder to help you write LINQ-like queries for custom collection

SQL type provider

This section explains how to use the `SqlDataConnection` (LINQ to SQL) type provider to generate types for the `Northwind` database. The SQL type provider reads the metadata information from the database and then generates SQL based on LINQ internally. We will walk through this using the SQL type provider in a step-by-step manner.

Preparing the test database

We will prepare the database using the SQL **Server Explorer** option of Visual Studio. On a server or local machine with SQL Express, we need to run through the following steps:

1. Use the `Northwind.sql` script provided in the examples of this book. Alternatively, download the `Northwind` SQL script file from `https://northwind database.codeplex.com/releases/view/71634`.
2. Open SQL **Server Explorer** in Visual Studio.
3. Create a new database called `Northwind`.
4. Choose **New Query…** and copy/paste the SQL script from the `Northwind.sql` file.
5. Run the SQL script to generate the database.
6. At the end, we can see a listing similar to the following screenshot:

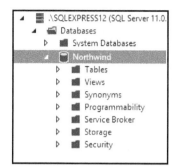

Using the type provider

Perform the following steps to use the SQL type provider:

1. Let's start by working on the type provider by creating an F# script file (exploratory programming!). First, we will set up the script file to reference the proper assemblies and namespaces. Let's use the following source code:

```
#r "FSharp.Data.TypeProviders"
#r "System.Data.Linq.dll"

open System
open System.Data
open System.Data.Linq
open Microsoft.FSharp.Data.TypeProviders
```

2. The next step is to initialize a type that will hold the reference of the actual type provider. In general, the type providers will be of the following syntax:

```
type <Name> = TypeProvider<....>
```

3. We can create the SQL type provider using the `SqlDataConnection` class with a static-generic parameter that accepts a connection string as follows:

```
type NorthwindDbSchema = SqlDataConnection<"Data Source=
<SERVER_NAME>;Initial Catalog=Northwind;Integrated
Security=True">
```

Replace the <SERVER_NAME> parameter with your reference to the SQL server that was used to prepare the database.

4. We will now get a reference of the underlying data context that LINQ to SQL uses for query generation:

```
let northwindDB = NorthwindDbSchema.GetDataContext()
northwindDB.DataContext.Log = System.Console.Out
```

We now have an object reference, `northwindDB`, that has the following items:

- Properties as table names:
    - The type of each of the properties is the same type of the corresponding column in the table, and these are generated by the F# type provider
- The types themselves appear in `northwindDB.ServiceTypes`
- We have also set the `Log` property of the `DataContext` class to visualize how the LINQ query is generated by the SQL type provider

Let's try to verify the type of the `Products` table:

```
> let products = northwindDB.Products
val products : Table<NorthwindDbSchema.ServiceTypes.Products>
```

By executing the preceding code in the F# interactive window, we can see the referenced type for the table that is generated under `ServiceTypes`. The compiler will create a type for all the tables or views present in the database.

Querying the data

We will now use the LINQ syntax to generate queries on the types. This is similar to what we saw in Chapter 4, *Imperative Programming in F#*, about using LINQ expressions:

1. Create a query to iterate the `Products` table, as follows:

```
let pQuery =
    query {
            for p in northwindDB.Products do
            select p
    }

pQuery |> Seq.iter(fun prod -> printfn "%d; %s" prod.ProductID
prod.ProductName)
```

2. Executing this quickly in the interactive window gives us the following results:

```
1; Chai
2; Chang
3; Aniseed Syrup
4; Chef Anton's Cajun Seasoning
5; Chef Anton's Gumbo Mix
```

3. We can also add all the different LINQ query operators on top of this type and see it working, as shown in the following code snippet:

```
let pWQuery =
    query {
            for p in northwindDB.Products do
            where (p.UnitPrice.Value > 15m)
        }
pWQuery |> Seq.iter(fun prod -> printfn "%d; %s; %A"
prod.ProductID prod.ProductName prod.UnitPrice)
```

4. Executing the preceding code snippet in the interactive window produces the following output:

```
1; Chai; 18.0000M
2; Chang; 19.0000M
4; Chef Anton's Cajun Seasoning; 22.0000M
5; Chef Anton's Gumbo Mix; 21.3500M
6; Grandma's Boysenberry Spread; 25.0000M
7; Uncle Bob's Organic Dried Pears; 30.0000M
```

Usually, database tables also have nullable columns, that is, columns that allow empty values. Nulls are imperative definitions the F# language supports inside of the query { ... } operator. In the preceding sample query, we used a nullable field in the where query. F# also provides several LINQ-related nullable operators in the Linq.NullableOperators module, such as comparison operators that work on nullable fields. For example, >? is a greater-than operator with a nullable value on the right. According to these operators, if either side of the expression is null, the evaluation returns as false.

Similarly, we can use all the different combinations of LINQ queries that we saw in Chapter 4, *Imperative Programming in F#*.

SQL entity type provider

The entity type provider uses **Entity Framework (EF)** to work with the database. EF is an **object-relational mapping (ORM)** tool to model database objects such as SQL tables with .NET-compatible types. In this section, you will learn how to use EF with the F# SQL entity type provider.

Similar to what we saw in the SQL type provider section, we will prepare a `NorthwindDB` for testing.

Using the type provider

We will use the EF **Code First** approach to work with the database. EF Code First is a set of conventions that allows us to represent our data models and directly write the code without having to use other tools such as UML. First, we will set up a simple F# script file to explore the SQL entity type provider. Add the following code to start exploring **LINQ to Entities**:

```
#r "System.Data.Entity.dll"
#r "FSharp.Data.TypeProviders"

open System
open System.Data
open System.Data.EntityClient
open Microsoft.FSharp.Data.TypeProviders

type EntityConnection =
SqlEntityConnection<ConnectionString="Server
=[<SERVER_NAME>];Initial Catalog=Northwind;Integrated
Security=SSPI;MultipleActiveResultSets=true",Pluralize = true>
let northwindEntities = EntityConnection.GetDataContext()
```

Replace <SERVER_NAME> with your reference to the SQL server that was used to prepare the database.

In the connection string, we will also use `MultipleActiveResultSets=true`, which means we can execute multiple commands asynchronously as supported in the EF.

Querying the data

Again, we will use the `query { .. }` expression to generate LINQ syntaxes and let LINQ to Entities deal with translating the expression into SQL. If we already know LINQ, it is simple to reuse our knowledge using LINQ in F# and apply it in all these different scenarios:

1. Create a query to iterate the `Products` table, as follows:

   ```
   let pQuery =
       query {
               for p in northwindDB.Products do
               select p
       }

   pQuery |> Seq.iter(fun prod -> printfn "%d; %s; %A"
   prod.ProductID prod.ProductName prod.UnitPrice)
   ```

2. Executing the same query we did with LINQ to SQL here also results in the same output:

   ```
   >
   1; Chai; 18.0000M
   2; Chang; 19.0000M
   3; Aniseed Syrup; 10.0000M
   4; Chef Anton's Cajun Seasoning; 22.0000M
   5; Chef Anton's Gumbo Mix; 21.3500M
   6; Grandma's Boysenberry Spread; 25.0000M
   7; Uncle Bob's Organic Dried Pears; 30.0000M
   8; Northwoods Cranberry Sauce; 40.0000M
   9; Mishi Kobe Niku; 97.0000M
   10; Ikura; 31.0000M
   . . .
   . . .
   ```

Likewise, all the functionality that is normally supported in EF can be realized using the SQL entity type provider.

OData type provider

OData is an open data protocol to allow the creation and consumption of queryable and interoperable REST APIs so we can interact with a data source through the Internet using simple HTTP requests, almost as if it were a local database. We will use the OData type provider to first explore the OData data from a particular source.

Prerequisites

We will set up our F# script file by referencing the proper OData and type provider assemblies:

1. Create an F# script file, `ODataTypeProviderSample.fsx`.
2. Add related references to the script file:

```
#r "FSharp.Data.TypeProviders"
#r "System.Data.Services.Client.dll"

open System
open System.Linq
open System.Data
open Microsoft.FSharp.Data.TypeProviders
```

Using the type provider

For this sample, we will not create or host an OData service itself, but we will use an existing `Northwind` OData service that is available at the following URL:

`http://services.odata.org/Northwind/Northwind.svc/`

We will declare a type with `ODataService` and get the following context:

```
type northwindOData =
ODataService<"http://services.odata.org/Northwind/Northwind.svc/">
let db = northwindOData.GetDataContext()
```

We can look at the different lists that are exposed from this OData service through the following screenshot:

OData supports only the following subset of query operations:

- `select`: This performs a projection on the entities
- `where`: This filters the entities
- `skip`: This identifies a subset of entities from a collection of entities
- `take`: This performs paging on the entities
- `orderBy`: This orders the collection of entities
- `thenBy`: This sorts the entities

There are some additional operations, such as `AddQueryOption` and `Expand`, which are very specific to OData.

Querying the data

With the supported OData query operations, we can explore the following queries using the `query { ... }` operators:

1. Specify fields in the `select` query, as shown in the following piece of code:

```
let pQuery =
    query {
            for p in db.Products do
            select p
    }

pQuery |> Seq.iter(fun prod -> printfn "%d; %s; %A"
```

```
prod.ProductID prod.ProductName prod.UnitPrice)
```

2. Executing the preceding code produces the following output in the interactive window:

```
1; Chai; 18.0000M
2; Chang; 19.0000M
3; Aniseed Syrup; 10.0000M
4; Chef Anton's Cajun Seasoning; 22.0000M
5; Chef Anton's Gumbo Mix; 21.3500M
. . .
. . .
```

3. Specify conditions in the `where` clause, as shown in the following code snippet:

```
let pWQuery =
    query {
            for p in db.Products do
            where (p.UnitPrice.Value > 25.0m)
        }
pWQuery |> Seq.iter(fun prod -> printfn "%d; %s; %A"
prod.ProductID prod.ProductName prod.UnitPrice)
```

4. Executing the preceding code snippet will result in the following output in the interactive window:

```
7; Uncle Bob's Organic Dried Pears; 30.0000M
8; Northwoods Cranberry Sauce; 40.0000M
9; Mishi Kobe Niku; 97.0000M
10; Ikura; 31.0000M
12; Queso Manchego La Pastora; 38.0000M
17; Alice Mutton; 39.0000M
18; Carnarvon Tigers; 62.5000M
. . .
. . .
```

5. Use different combinations in the query, as shown in the following code snippet:

```
let pWQuery2 =
    query {
            for p in db.Products do
            where (p.ProductName.Contains("C"))
        }
pWQuery2 |> Seq.iter(fun prod -> printfn "%d; %s; %A"
```

```
prod.ProductID
prod.ProductName prod.UnitPrice)
```

6. Executing the preceding query in the interactive window will produce the following output:

```
1; Chai; 18.0000M
2; Chang; 19.0000M
4; Chef Anton's Cajun Seasoning; 22.0000M
5; Chef Anton's Gumbo Mix; 21.3500M
7; Uncle Bob's Organic Dried Pears; 30.0000M
8; Northwoods Cranberry Sauce; 40.0000M
11; Queso Cabrales; 21.0000M
...
...
```

The OData type provider doesn't support the latest changes in OData 4.0, so do check which version of OData you are connecting to before using this type provider.

Web service type provider

The web service type provider works with **Web Service Definition Language** (**WSDL**), an XML specification for describing network services. Support for WSDL is there in the .NET framework with the `SvcUtil.exe` code generation utility. The web service type provider uses this utility to generate the types and exposes them to F# via the type provider. We will follow the same steps as our earlier examples by creating an F# script file and doing an exploratory analysis of the underlying data source.

Prerequisites

We will set up our F# script file by referencing the proper OData and the type provider assemblies.

1. Create an F# script file, `WSDLTypeProviderSample.fsx`.
2. Add related references to the script file, as follows:

```
#r "FSharp.Data.TypeProviders"
#r "System.Runtime.Serialization.dll"
#r "System.ServiceModel.dll"
open System
open System.ServiceModel
open Microsoft.FSharp.Linq
```

```
open Microsoft.FSharp.Data.TypeProviders
```

Using the type provider

We will use the **Terra** web service to query and explore the web service types. We will use the following code to initialize the type provider:

```
type TerraService =
WsdlService<"http://msrmaps.com/TerraService2.asmx?WSDL">
let db = TerraService.GetTerraServiceSoap()
```

We can explore the different functions that this service exposes:

Querying the data

Each web service will have its own generated types. We will try to resolve the latitude/longitude point based on a given address, as follows:

```
try
    let place = new
    TerraService.ServiceTypes.msrmaps.com.Place(City =
    "Bangalore", State = "Karnataka", Country = "India")
    let latlng = db.ConvertPlaceToLonLatPt(place)
    printfn "London Geo Location : %A" latlng
with
```

```
    | :? ServerTooBusyException as e ->
        printfn "Server Busy Exception: %A" e

    | e -> printfn "Exception: %A" e
```

It is also important to note that we wrap up the functionality with exception blocks in case there is a delay in the web service to respond back.

Data analysis with type providers

The World Bank is an international organization that provides financial and technical assistance to developing countries around the world. The World Bank provides data indicators and other data about countries around the world. There are about 8,000 indicators that can be accessed in the World Bank database. We will use this data to do some analytics/charting.

The World Bank data can be accessed via a type provider available specifically for the World Bank in the `FSharp.Data` library (this is available via **NuGet**, a repository for .NET libraries). We will then use the `FSharp.Charting` library to visualize the data in a chart and see some indicators.

 NuGet libraries can be accessed either by the NuGet tool itself (`https://www.nuget.org/`) or **Paket**, another package manager with very good integration and the most used F# development tools (`https://fspro jects.github.io/Paket/`).

Prerequisites

We will set up our F# script file by referencing the `FSharp.Data` and `FSharp.Charting` libraries:

1. Create an F# script file, `WorldBankTypeProvider.fsx`.

2. Add related references to the script file, as follows:

```
#r @"../packages/FSharp.Data.2.2.0/lib/net40/FSharp.Data.dll"
#I @"../packages/FSharp.Charting.0.90.9"
#load "FSharp.Charting.fsx"

open FSharp.Data
open FSharp.Charting
open Microsoft.FSharp.Linq
```

We will use the `FSharp.Charting.fsx` library from the NuGet package reference as it has the helper classes to render the chart on script execution.

Using the type provider

Firstly, we will get the World Bank object and try to access the different indicators that it exposes. This is a very easy way to understand in an exploratory way, just like we saw earlier with the default type providers:

```
let data = WorldBankData.GetDataContext()
let gdp2010 =
    data.Countries
        .``United States``
        .Indicators
        .``GDP (current US$)``
        .[2010]
```

The preceding code snippet shows how to access the World Bank context, and we see a strongly typed way to access the **gross domestic product** (**GDP**) indicator for the United States:

```
let data = WorldBankData.GetDataContext()
data.Countries
    .``United States``
    .Indicators
    .GDP    I
    🔧 Average grace period on new external debt commitments, private (years)
    🔧 Average grant element on new external debt commitments, private (%)
    🔧 GDP (constant 2005 US$)
    🔧 GDP (constant LCU)
    🔧 GDP (current LCU)
    🔧 GDP (current US$)
    🔧 GDP deflator (base year varies by country)
    🔧 GDP growth (annual %)
    🔧 GDP per capita (constant 2005 US$)
```

Now, let's try to get the GDP values for two years, and then compare them using charts:

```
let gdp2006 = countries |> Array.map(fun c -> c.Name,
c.Indicators.``GDP
(current US$)``.[2006])
let gdp2011 = countries |> Array.map(fun c -> c.Name,
c.Indicators.``GDP
(current US$)``.[2011])
```

We will use the FSharp.Charting library to define a line chart with both the GDP **key performance indicators** (**KPIs**), as shown in the following code lines:

```
Chart.Combine(
    [ Chart.Line(gdp2006, Name = "GDP 2006")
      Chart.Line(gdp2011, "GDP 2011")  ])
```

The FSharp.Charting.fsx file has the required functionality to show the output of the data rendered as a chart. After executing the preceding code snippet, we can see the output as the following chart:

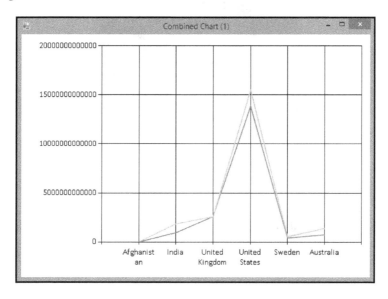

A pie chart gives us a comparative visualization over the different GDPs of the countries. The same GDP data can be visualized as a pie chart with the following code:

```
Chart.Pie(gdp2006, Name = "GDP 2006")
```

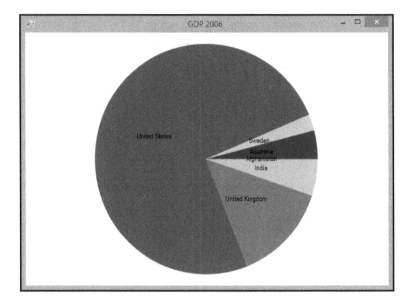

The sample code is also available in the source project; feel free to play around and explore the data with charting.

Query builder

The query builder allows use to write LINQ-like queries within `query { ... }` code blocks. The F# LINQ expressions have all the functions defined in the `QueryBuilder` class. We can also define our own query builder and use the `CustomOperation` attribute to define new LINQ operations. The need to build a custom query builder is required when we have a new set of functions that is not available in the existing `QueryBuilder` class, or if we want to have custom functions for data collections.

In this section, we will learn how to create a custom sequence builder to reuse the `Seq` module as LINQ query expressions. The query expression needs to satisfy three preconditions, which are as follows:

- `For`: This is the method used to support the F# query syntax. It projects each element of a sequence to another sequence and combines the resulting sequences into one.
- `Yield`: This returns a sequence of length, one which contains the specified value.
- `Zero`: This returns an empty sequence of the given type.

All these three functions are required by the query expression to translate from F# to LINQ properly. Let's take a look at how to create a custom sequence builder:

1. Implement the sequence builder by defining the required class and methods:

```
open System
open System.Linq
open Microsoft.FSharp.Linq

type SeqBuilder() =

    member x.For(source: seq<'t>, body: 't -> seq<'v>) =
        seq { for v in source do yield! body v }

    member x.Yield (item: 't) : seq<'t> = seq { yield item }
    member x.Zero () = Seq.empty

    [<CustomOperation("select")>]
    member x.Select(source: seq<'t>, f: 't -> 'v) : seq<'v> =
        Seq.map f source

let myseq = new SeqBuilder()
```

2. In this class, we have implemented the required `For`, `Yield`, and `Zero` functions to use the query expressions. There is also a `Select` function that implements the `Seq.map` functionality. We can use the sequence builder as follows:

```
let x =
    myseq {
        for i in 1..10 do
        select (fun i -> i + 10)
    }
```

3. The `select` projection requires a function to be passed in the LINQ statement. We can improve the `select` function by adding the `ProjectionParameter` attribute, which will help resolve the projection function by the compiler automatically. We will change the `select` function as follows:

```
[<CustomOperation("select")>]
member x.Select(source: seq<'t>, [<ProjectionParameter>] f: 't
 -> 'v) :
seq<'v> =
    Seq.map f source
```

4. Now we can use the `select` operation as mentioned in the following code snippet:

```
let x1 =
    myseq {
            for i in 1..10 do
            select (i + 10)
    }
```

5. In C#, we can define variables inside LINQ statements that hold onto some state during the operation. We can define a variable space in an F# query statement by marking the `CustomOperation` attribute with the `MaintainsVariableSpace=true` property as well:

```
[<CustomOperation("sort", MaintainsVariableSpace=true)>]
member x.Sort (source: seq<'t>) =
    Seq.sort source
```

6. Usage of our custom sequence builder is shown in the following code snippet:

```
> myseq {
        let x = 1
        for i in 1 .. 10 do
        sort
        select (x, i+10)
    };;
val it : (int * int) seq =
  [|(1, 11); (1, 12); (1, 13); (1, 14); (1, 15); (1, 16); (1,
    17); (1, 18); (1, 19); (1, 20)|]
```

There are several other properties in the `CustomOperationAttribute` class that help in implementing complex LINQ statements, which are as follows:

Member	Description
AllowIntoPattern	This indicates whether the custom operation supports the use of the `into` pattern immediately after the use of the operation or another computation expression to consume the results of the operation.
IsLikeGroupJoin	This indicates whether the custom operation is similar to a `join` group in a sequence computation. The operation supports two inputs with a correlation constraint and generates a group.
IsLikeJoin	This indicates whether the custom operation is similar to a `join` operation in a sequence computation.
IsLikeZip	This indicates whether the custom operation is similar to a ZIP in a sequence computation.
JoinConditionWord	This indicates the name used for an `on` keyword in the query operator.
MaintainsVariableSpace	This indicates whether the custom operation maintains a variable space in the query or computation expression.
MaintainsVariableSpaceUsingBind	This indicates whether the custom operation maintains the variable space of the query or computation expression through the use of the `bind` operation.
Name	This is the name of the custom operator or the computation expression.

Summary

In this chapter, we covered some type providers that are available in the F# language and explored how to use them. We also saw how the query { ... } operators can be customized to use custom builders for ease of use. Together with other F# features such as type inference or the F# interactive environment, type providers are a fantastic way to do exploratory programming as we can start coding with very low ceremony, and investigate the data source directly from F# using the IDE autocompletion.

In the next chapter, you will learn how to create a web application using F# on both the server and client sides.

7
Web Programming in F#

The modern web has three main requirements: it must be responsive, scalable, and deal with tons of data. Features such as asynchronous workflows, composability, or data tools make F# a perfect fit for web programming. In this chapter, we will review the most common tools used for web development with F# and see the benefits they bring to the table to decide which one is the most appropriate for our use case.

You will learn how to build web servers using some of the most common .NET libraries for this purpose, which are as follows:

- **ASP.NET Web API**: Thanks to its convention-based HTTP route bindings, it is very easy to build web services in F# using ASP.NET Web API, also remaining in the comfort of Microsoft tooling for web development.
- **Suave**: This is a web server specifically designed to take full advantage of F# and functional programming characteristics. Instead of controllers, as with ASP.NET, Suave defines routes using function composition, which gives you greater flexibility and makes it much easier to reuse your code, as simple functions are much more composable than class declarations.

 It's also possible to create ASP.NET MVC projects in F#. However, the process is somewhat convoluted and the framework does not take much advantage of F# characteristics. For these reasons, we will not cover ASP.NET MVC in this chapter.

Even if F# is traditionally considered a server-side language, we will review the following tools that allow us to write code for the browser in F#:

- **Websharper**: This is a full framework to develop web applications both on the server and client side with idiomatic F# in a type-safe manner.

• **Fable**: When you need to stay closer to JavaScript and its numerous libraries and development tools, but still want the full power of F#, Fable is the best choice. Fable is a lightweight F# to JavaScript compiler designed to bring together the best of the two languages and their ecosystem.

ASP.NET Web API 2

In 2013, Microsoft developed a framework within the range of ASP.NET tools to easily create REST APIs. The aim was to minimize the boilerplate needed to create web service controllers. While the design is mainly aimed at an object-oriented language such as C#, its simplicity makes it possible to adapt it to F# without any complication.

In ASP.NET Web API, you can set HTTP routes and verbs automatically by defining a type with the appropriate names and attributes. The use of attributes in .NET is frequent for libraries that use reflection to map .NET types to other data, such as Newtonsoft.Json or sqlite-net, but ASP.NET Web API also makes use of naming conventions to prevent pollution of your code with too many attributes.

This is what a hello world example looks like in ASP.NET Web API 2:

```
type HelloController() =
    inherit System.Web.Http.ApiController()
    member x.Get(name: string) = sprintf "Hello %s!" name
```

In a properly set Web API 2 app, this automatically creates a hello HTTP route in our host that accepts GET calls, including a name parameter, as shown in the following code line:

```
http://localhost/hello/John -> returns "Hello John!"
```

As you can see, this is done by convention. The route is taken from the name of the controller type, and the HTTP verb and the parameter from the signature of the method.

Web API 2 is a good way to write web servers in F# while remaining in the ASP.NET ecosystem and getting the most out of Visual Studio tooling. However, in this chapter, as its main target is the C# language, we will focus on Suave, another web server specifically designed for F#. If you are more interested in Web API 2, please check the extensive documentation on the MicrosoftASP.NET website (`https://www.asp.net/`).

Suave

While ASP.NET Web API is very convenient, you can see it is mainly designed for an **object-oriented programming** (**OOP**) language as we will map our HTTP routes and verb using classes and methods. This makes it a bit more difficult to create reusable components using simple functions as it is common in F#.

Suave (`https://suave.io`) is a web server that is very popular within the F# community and is specifically designed to take full advantage of the F# features. Suave is a lightweight, non-blocking web server. The non-blocking I/O model is efficient and suitable to build fast and scalable network applications.

The following is a brief list of advantages of using Suave:

- It is asynchronous by default
- Its routes are built using composable functions
- It includes common tools for web development–HTTPS, authentication, keep-alive, and compression
- It is cross-platform, which means it works on Linux, OS X, and Windows
- It can be embedded in other applications
- It can be used from an F# script

Unlike desktop applications that most of the time only have one single user, web applications must be prepared to respond to many users at any given time. Because of this, it is very important that a single request does not block the whole server. This is why costly operations (for example, writing to a database) must be done asynchronously, meaning that the main thread of the application is free to respond to other users while the current request finishes. To achieve this, all the functions to handle requests in Suave must return an F# `Async` object. This way, the developer can be sure there is not a single point in the app that will act as a performance bottleneck.

As you can see, simplicity is one of Suave's premises. Suave does not require any installation; it is just a .dll assembly that you need to reference from your code. In fact, you can start a web server using an **F# Interactive** window with this minimal script:

```
#r "packages/Suave/lib/net40/Suave.dll"
open Suave
startWebServer defaultConfig (Successful.OK "Hello World!")
```

This will start a web server on default port 8083, which responds with "Hello World!" to any request.

Routing with Suave

Routes are the reaming part of the URL after removing the server address. In the past, it was common that URLs pointed directly to a .html file. However, today, routes commonly are just abstract entry points that determine how the web app will respond to the request, and sometimes they may even carry some data through parameters.

Modern web applications are usually structured around their routes, which is why, to keep our code base flexible, it is important to be able to compose and refactor our routes easily.

Documentation in Suave is mostly written in the code itself, which is perfect for exploratory programming. Let's take a look at the signature of the startWebServer function:

```
val startWebServer : config:SuaveConfig -> webpart:WebPart -> unit
```

This means that, to start a web server, we will only need a configuration and WebPart, which is just a type alias for the following function type:

```
type WebPart = HttpContext -> Async<HttpContext option>
```

Moreover, as you already know by now, functions in F# can be easily composed by other functions. Let's take a deeper look at two interesting things in this signature: first, WebPart always return an Async value, and this is why Suave can boast about itself as a non-blocking server. All requests must be handled using F# asynchronous workflows, and thus the server will not be unresponsive when working on expensive operations such as database access. Second, the result of this asynchronous computation is an HttpContext option. This allows the functions to return None, to yield control to another component. Let's see a practical example of this:

```
open Suave
open Suave.Operators
let app =
  choose [
```

```
        Filters.GET >=> Successful.OK "Hello GET"
        Filters.POST >=> Successful.OK "Hello POST" ]
    startWebServer defaultConfig app
```

Suave uses the `>=>` operator to chain async options. If the first operand returns `None`, the operation will be short-circuited and the second operand will not run. This keeps Suave performant (no needless operations will be executed). In our example, the `GET` filter will detect if we are dealing with an HTTP `GET` call. If this is not the case, the program will jump directly to the second filter, `POST`.

The following are the other useful Suave combinators:

- `choose`: This executes, one by one, a list of `WebParts` until one of them returns `Some`. It is useful to build route trees.
- `OK`: This combinator always succeeds and writes its argument to the underlying response stream using the HTTP code 200. There are other combinators in the `Suave.Successful` namespace to use other codes such as `ACCEPTED` (202) or `CREATED` (201). Likewise, the `Suave.RequestErrors` and `Suave.ServerErrors` namespaces contain combinators to return HTTP codes representing errors, such as `NOT_FOUND` (404) or `INTERNAL_ERROR` (500). Suave favors dealing with errors in a typed way (for example, returning `None` or an HTTP error code) instead of just throwing exceptions.

- `path`: This is used to match against a named route. Suave contains other utility methods such as `pathScan` to match arguments in the route in a typed manner (for example, to force a product ID to be an integer, use `pathScan "products/%i" (fun id -> OK (sprintf "Product %i" id))`) or `pathRegex` to match a regular expression against a given path.
- `context`: This is a convenience method to look into `HttpContext` and decide which `WebPart` to return. The synonym for `context` is `warbler`.
- `request`: This is another convenience method, same as `context`, but it only looks at the `HttpRequest` header.
- `authenticateBasic`: This is found within the `Suave.Authentication` namespace. It protects a route with HTTP basic authentication.

With these combinators, let's see an example of a slightlywant to display the nam more complex route tree:

```
open Suave
open Suave.Filters
open Suave.Operators
open Suave.Successful
```

```
let greet area (reqParams: (string * (string option)) list) =
    reqParams
    |> List.tryPick (fun (k,v) -> if k = "name" then v else None)
    |> function Some name -> name | None -> "World"
    |> sprintf "Hello from %s, %s!" area
let app =
    choose [
        path "/public" >=> choose [
            // Access the HttpRequest and check the query of form
            parameters
            GET >=> request(fun request -> greet "public"
            request.query |> OK)
            POST >=> request(fun request -> greet "public"
            request.form |> OK)
        ]
        // This route is protected by HTTP Basic Authentication
        path "/private" >=> Authentication.authenticateBasic
            (fun (username, password) -> username = "me" &&
            password = "abc")
            (choose [
                GET >=> request(fun request -> greet "private"
                request.query |> OK)
                POST >=> request(fun request -> greet "private"
                request.form |> OK)
            ])
        RequestErrors.NOT_FOUND "Found no handlers"
    ]
startWebServer defaultConfig app
```

Templating with Suave

You can use Suave with the **DotLiquid** render engine. DotLiquid is an HTML template render engine based in **Liquid** syntax, wherein templates are rendered by passing an object model and using it to replace Liquid code with generated HTML. Let's say we have an F# record to represent a teacher such as { Name: string; Students: string list }. We will use double curly braces to access a property of the model, as shown in the following code lines:

```
<h1>Teacher: {{model.Name}}</h1>
```

The preceding Liquid code gets converted into following:

```
<h1>Teacher: Sarah</h1>
```

Liquid tags, denoted by curly braces and percent signs, are used for logic and control flow, as shown in the following example:

```
<ul>
  {% for item in model.Students %}
    <li>{{ item }}</li>
  {% endfor %}
</ul>
```

The preceding Liquid code gets converted into the following:

```
<ul>
    <li>Peter</li>
    <li>Linda</li>
    <li>Mariah</li>
</ul>
```

Liquid also admits filters, which can change the output of a Liquid object. For example, if we want to display the names of the students in uppercase, we will write the following line of code (note the vertical separator between the Liquid object and the filter):

```
<li>{{ item | upcase }}</li>
```

Now, let's write a minimum example of serving an HTML page rendered from a Liquid template. After we have added Suave, DotLiquid, and the `Suave.DotLiquid` packages, we can use an `.fsx` script as follows:

```
#r "packages/Suave/lib/net40/Suave.dll"
#r "packages/DotLiquid/lib/NET40/DotLiquid.dll"
#r "packages/Suave.DotLiquid/lib/net40/Suave.DotLiquid.dll"
open Suave
open Suave.Filters
open Suave.Operators
type Teacher = { Name: string; Students: string list }

let model = { Name="Sarah"; Students=["Peter"; "Linda"; "Mariah"]}

DotLiquid.setTemplatesDir(__SOURCE_DIRECTORY__)
let app = choose [
 path "/" >=> DotLiquid.page ("template.html") model
 ]
startWebServer defaultConfig app
```

Provided we have a `template.html` file in the same directory as the script similar to the following piece of code:

```html
<!DOCTYPE html>
<html>
  <head>
    <meta charset="utf-8">
    <title>My Liquid template</title>
  </head>
  <body>
    <h1>Teacher: {{ model.Name }}</h1>
    <ul>
      {% for item in model.Students %}
        <li>{{ item | upcase }}</li>
      {% endfor %}
    </ul>
  </body>
</html>
```

Suave also includes a DSL to render HTML views on the server side. To use it, you will need to install the NuGet `Suave.Experimental` package, and then you will be able to build your templates directly in the F# code. When using `Suave.Html` DSL, the preceding example will become as follows:

```
#r "packages/Suave/lib/net40/Suave.dll"
#r "packages/Suave.Experimental/lib/net40/Suave.Experimental.dll"
open Suave
open Suave.Filters
open Suave.Operators
open Suave.Successful
open Suave.Html
type Teacher = { Name: string; Students: string list }

let model = { Name="Sarah"; Students=["Peter"; "Linda"; "Mariah"]}

let page (model: Teacher) =
    html [
        head [ title "Suave HTML" ]
        body [
            tag "h1" [] (text model.Name)
            tag "ul" [] (flatten
                [for item in model.Students do
                    yield tag "li" [] (item.ToUpper() |> text)]
            )
        ]
    ] |> xmlToString
let app =
```

```
        choose [
            path "/" >=> OK (page model)
        ]
    startWebServer defaultConfig app
```

The advantage of this approach is that you can use all the power of F# and .NET classes to generate your templates. In the preceding example, we used an F# list comprehension to build the student list, and displaying the names in uppercase is as simple as calling the `ToUpper` string method. Also, as usual with F#, reusing and composing parts of your code becomes trivial, so you can refactor any repetitive code to a helper function.

Please note that the DSL is still experimental and subject to change. Because of this, there is not much documentation yet, but you can check the code at `https://github.com/SuaveIO` `/suave/tree/master/src/Experimental`.

WebSharper

WebSharper is a full web framework that allows you to use F# not only on the server but on the client side too. WebSharper also includes many extensions to interact with other libraries or environments, such as mobile phones, and takes full advantage of F# composability and reusability capabilities. However, one of the main features of WebSharper is that it takes F# type safety to the next level to catch many errors at compile time, including safe URLs.

Installing WebSharper

The easiest way to install WebSharper is to use the extensions available for Visual Studio and Xamarin Studio. You can download them from its website and follow the instructions to create a new WebSharper project at `http://websharper.com/downloads`.

WebSharper includes a set of opinionated tools, allowing users to quickly develop websites without worrying about boilerplate. Here, we will briefly overview some of these tools.

Sitelets

WebSharper Sitelets provides you with an easy way to create type-safe websites with HTTP route resolution and HTML rendering. These websites can also be composed to form more complex sites from simple and manageable pieces. Route resolution just involves defining an F# union type containing our endpoints, similar to the following example:

```
type EndPoint =
    | Index
    | Student of name: string
```

HTML rendering is similar to the Suave DSL we saw in the preceding section, and can be done directly in the F# code, as shown in the following example:

```
let IndexContent (model: Teacher) context : Async<Content<EndPoint>> =
        Content.Page(
            Title = "My WebSharper Template",
            Body = [
                h1 [text model.Name]
                ul [for item in model.Students do
                        yield li [text item] :> Doc]
            ])
```

This way, an example similar to the one we saw in the preceding section for Suave can be expressed as follows in WebSharper:

```
open WebSharper
open WebSharper.Sitelets
open WebSharper.UI.Next
open WebSharper.UI.Next.Html
type Teacher = { Name: string; Students: string list }
let model = { Name="Sarah"; Students=["Peter"; "Linda"; "Mariah"]}
type EndPoint =
    | Index
    | Student of name: string
let IndexContent (model: Teacher) context :
Async<Content<EndPoint>> =
    Content.Page(
        Title = "My WebSharper Template",
        Body = [
            h1 [text model.Name]
            ul [for item in model.Students do
                    yield li [text item] :> Doc]
        ])
[<Website>]
let MySampleWebsite : Sitelet<EndPoint> =
    Sitelet.Content "/Index" EndPoint.Index (IndexContent model)
```

Notice how we have manually mapped "/Index" to the function that will generate the HTML page in the last line. However, one of the most interesting features is that we can infer safe URLs directly from the EndPoint type definition. For this, we will only need to replace the last value with the following code snippet:

```
[<Website>]
let MySampleWebsite : Sitelet<EndPoint> =
    Sitelet.Infer (fun context action ->
        match action with
        | Index -> IndexContent model context
        | Student name -> failwith "Not yet implemented"
    )
```

The Sitelet.Infer function will automatically create two URL routes based on our EndPoint definition: "/Index" and "/Student" (we will implement the last one further down the chapter). Furthermore, the second URL will accept a string parameter to indicate the name of the student, such as "/Student/Peter". The default behavior of Sitelet.Infer may not fit our requirements. For example, we may want to match IndexContent to the root path. In this case, we can use special attributes in the EndPoint type definition, as follows:

```
type EndPoint =
    | [<EndPoint "/">] Index
    | Student of name: string
```

You can find more information about these attributes in the WebSharper documentation. One of the most interesting things about Sitelets' URL inferring capability is that we can use it in the HTML templates to create safe links. We will modify the preceding IndexContent function to include a link to each student's page as follows:

```
let IndexContent (model: Teacher) context :
Async<Content<EndPoint>> =
    let createLink studentName =
        // When adding Attr suffix, functions will also accept an
attribute list
        aAttr [context.Link (Student studentName) |> attr.href]
            [text studentName]
    Content.Page(
        Title = "My WebSharper Template",
        Body = [
            h1 [text model.Name]
            ul [for item in model.Students do
                    yield li [createLink item] :> Doc]
        ])
```

The `context.Link` helper will automatically generate URLs, such as `"/Student/Peter"` and so on, as per the URL inferring of the `EndPoint` definition. This means that if we decide to change the URL for this page, the template will correct itself with no further effort. No more broken links!

UI.Next

The helper functions we were using above to build the HTML template (`h1`, `ul`, and so on) actually belong to the `WebSharper.UI.Next` library. The `UI.Next` library is not only for building static HTML pages; it allows interactivity on the client side too.

To understand how reactivity works in `UI.Next`, we will need to learn the following two concepts:

- **Reactive variables**: These are values that can be set imperatively, similar to F# `ref`.
- **Reactive views**: These are values that depend on other nodes, either reactive variables or views, in the `UI.Next` data flow graph. They cannot be set imperatively. Instead, its value is always determined by the node the view depends on.

Both reactive variables and views can be associated with an element of the HTML DOM. We will review our preceding sample to add a filter for the student names. For this, we will only need to modify `IndexContent`, as shown in the following code block:

```
let IndexContent (model: Teacher) context : Async<Content<EndPoint>> =
    let createLink studentName =
        aAttr [context.Link (Student studentName) |> attr.href]
              [text studentName]
    let filterVar = Var.Create ""
    let studentsView =
        filterVar.View
        |> View.Map (fun filter ->
            let filter = filter.ToUpper()
            model.Students
            |> Seq.filter (fun name ->
                name.ToLower().Contains(filter))
            |> Seq.map (fun name -> li [createLink name] :> Doc)
            |> ul
        )
    Content.Page(
        Title = "My WebSharper Template",
        Body = [
```

```
h1 [text model.Name]
div [
    Doc.Input [] filterVar
    Doc.EmbedView studentsView
]
])
```

Note that we are creating a reactive variable, `filterVar`, whose initial value is just an empty string. From it, we will generate a view using the `View` property, and then we will map this view to another one that creates an unordered HTML list of students, but this time filtered by the value of `filterVar`. With the reactive variable and view in place, we will only need to modify our template by replacing the static list with an input field bound to `filterVar`, and the `studentsView` variable directly embedded into the DOM. To associate the reactive variables and view with the DOM elements, we will use the methods of the `Doc` namespace. In the preceding code example, `Doc.Input` directly binds the content of the HTML input field, which is editable by the user, to our `filterVar`. Whenever the value of `filterVar` changes, `studentsView`, which is directly embedded into the DOM thanks to `Doc.EmbedView`, will change too.

There is more to WebSharper `UI.Next` that we can cover here, such as animations and Formlets. Please refer to the extensive available online for more information at `http://webs harper.com/docs`.

Fable

While WebSharper is a great way to use F# when building web apps both in the backend and frontend, sometimes we may need more flexibility when interacting with JavaScript. Fable is a lightweight F# to JavaScript compiler that does not provide any specific tool to build web apps. However, it allows you to interact with any modern JavaScript development tool and library, not only for the browser, but also for server apps with Node.js, desktop with GitHub Electron, or mobile with React Native or Fuse.

The experience of developing with Fable is a bit different from what we have seen so far, as one of its main guidelines is to stay as close as possible to the JavaScript ecosystem, not only during runtime but also while developing. For example, Fable itself is not distributed through NuGet, the usual repository for .NET libraries, but **Node Package Manager** (**npm**), a popular register and package manager forNode.js *Node.js* libraries and other JavaScript tools.

Let's see how we can create a hello world program in Fable. First of all, we will need to install the compiler on our machine. Fable is a mix of a .NET and a Node.js app, so we will need both frameworks in order to run it. If you do not have Node.js installed, you can easily download it from its website (`www.nodejs.org`). After running the installer, you will be able to use both the `node` and `npm` commands from the command line.

The npm packages can be installed both locally or globally. It is usual to install packages with a **command-line interpreter** (**CLI**) globally so we have direct access to them from our `PATH`. To do that with Fable, type the following on a terminal window:

```
npm install -g fable-compiler
```

 Note that the actual name of the npm package is `fable-compiler`, and we will use the `-g` argument to make the installation globally.

Now we can call the `fable` command from the terminal too. We will use it to compile a file containing the F# code. Just use any editor to type the following code and save it as `HelloWorld.fsx`:

```
printfn "Hello World!"
```

Once this is done, type the following on the terminal in the same directory as `HelloWorld.fsx`:

```
fable HelloWorld.fsx
```

This will generate the following `HelloWorld.js` file, which can be run with node:

```
node HelloWorld.js
```

After pressing the *return* key, you should see **Hello World!** on the screen. This may not look very exciting, but it means that we are running the F# code on a completely different platform than .NET. The JavaScript ecosystem has grown enormously in recent years, so Fable opens a new world of opportunities for F#!

In future chapters, we will learn how to use Fable to create desktop applications too. However, for now, we will focus on frontend web apps–the original purpose of the JavaScript language.

Using Fable with React

As mentioned in the preceding section, Fable doesn't include any specific tool by default to create web apps, but it allows you to take advantage of any modern JavaScript library. We will see how to create a simple **Single Page Application (SPA)** using **React**, a popular library to render HTML views directly on the client side. React uses a virtual DOM to minimize changes to the actual web page DOM, which is usually the performance bottleneck of most SPAs. In order to keep this virtual DOM efficient, React promotes the use immutable components. This way, anytime components are updated, React can quickly compare them against the virtual DOM using fast reference checks and apply no more patches that aren't necessary to the actual DOM.

React examples normally use a custom language named **JSX**, which combines JavaScript with HTML-like tags. Let's say we want to render a view, or a component, as they are called in React terminology, named CommentBox and mount it in the element of our page with ID content, we will write the following piece of code:

```
ReactDOM.render(
  <CommentBox url="/api/comments" pollInterval={2000} />,
  document.getElementById('content')
);
```

The url and pollInterval parameters are what React calls props. Think of them as the configuration objects of our component and note that, as commented in the preceding section, they are immutable and cannot be modified by the component. However, we will see later that these values can actually be updated by a parent view that propagates the changes to the children.

Fable does not use JSX but, thanks to the flexibility of F#, it incorporates a DSL with very similar results. The preceding code will become the following in pure F#:

```
ReactDom.render(
    R.com<CommentBox,_,_> {
    url = "/api/comments"
    pollInterval = 2000.
    } [],
    Browser.document.getElementById "content")
```

Now, let's adapt the example we can find in the React home page to create a simple to-do list in F# using Fable:

```
#r "../node_modules/fable-core/Fable.Core.dll"
#r "../node_modules/fable-react/Fable.React.dll"

open System
open Fable.Core
open Fable.Core.JsInterop
open Fable.Import
open Fable.Helpers.React.Props
module R=Fable.Helpers.React

type Todo =
    { id: DateTime; text: string }

// The PojoAttribute means the record will be
// compiled as a Plain JS Object, required by React
type [<Pojo>] TodoList =
    { items: Todo list; text: string }

type [<Pojo>] TodoAppProps =
    { url: string; pollInterval: float }

type TodoListView(props) =
    inherit React.Component<TodoList,obj>(props)

  member this.render() =
    let createItem (item: Todo) =
        R.li [Key (string item.id)]
            [R.str item.text]
    List.map createItem this.props.items
    |> R.ul []

type TodoAppView(props) =
    inherit React.Component<obj,TodoList>(props)
    do base.setInitState({ items = []; text = "" })

    member this.onChange(e: React.SyntheticEvent) =
        let newtext = unbox e.target?value
        { this.state with text = newtext }
        |> this.setState

    member this.handleSubmit(e: React.SyntheticEvent) =
        e.preventDefault()
        let newItem = {
            text = this.state.text
            id = DateTime.Now
```

```
        }
        let nextItems = this.state.items@[newItem]
        this.setState({ items = nextItems; text="" })

    member this.render() =
        let buttonText =
            this.state.items.Length + 1
            |> sprintf "Add #%i"
        R.div [] [
            R.h3 [] [R.str "TODO"]
            R.com<TodoListView,_,_> this.state []
            R.form [OnSubmit this.handleSubmit] [
                R.input [
                    OnChange this.onChange
                    Value (U2.Case1 this.state.text)
                ] []
                R.button [] [R.str buttonText]
            ]
        ]

ReactDom.render(
    R.com<TodoAppView,_,_> None [],
    Browser.document.getElementById "content")

ReactDom.render(
    R.com<TodoAppView,_,_> {
    url = "/api/comments"
    pollInterval = 2000.
    } [],
    Browser.document.getElementById "content")
```

Now we will go through the sample step by step. First, we will reference a couple of libraries containing helpers to use Fable and interact with React, respectively named `Fable.Core.dll` and `Fable.React.dll`. Like `fable-compiler`, these libraries are distributed through npm, so we will assume that they can be found in the `node_modules` directory, where npm puts the packages by default. In the next chapter, you will learn how to download npm packages in more detail.

After the references, we will open the appropriate modules to make the helper functions available, as shown in the following code block:

```
#r "node_modules/fable-core/Fable.Core.dll"
#r "node_modules/fable-react/Fable.React.dll"
open System
open Fable.Core
open Fable.Core.JsInterop
open Fable.Import
```

```
open Fable.Helpers.React.Props
module R=Fable.Helpers.React
```

 Note that this code is intended for a .fsx script. This way, we can include .dll references directly in the code.

Now we will define a simple React component that will hold our to-do items. The TodoListView function is a very simple component without logic that only contains the mandatory method for all React components, such as render. This method will be called whenever the component needs to be redrawn. Note how we use the Fable React helpers, such as R.ul or R.il, to represent DOM tags:

```
type TodoListView(props) =
    inherit React.Component<TodoList,obj>(props)
    member this.render() =
        let createItem (item: Todo) =
            R.li [Key (string item.id)] [
R.str item.text]
        R.ul [] (List.map createItem this.props.items)
```

After that comes the TodoAppView function, which is a slightly more complicated component as it contains state and logic to handle the events that will update the state and force a redraw of its child component, which is TodoListView. Note how we initialize the state by directly assigning it to the state property in the class constructor. However, after that, we will need to use the setState method, which is inherited from React.Component, whenever we need to update it:

```
type TodoAppView(props)
as this =
    inherit React.Component<obj,TodoList>(props)
    do this.state <- { items = []; text =
"" }
    member this.onChange (e: React.SyntheticEvent) =
        this.setState({ this.state with text = unbox e.target?value
})
    member this.handleSubmit (e: React.SyntheticEvent) =
        e.preventDefault()
        let nextItems = this.state.items@[{ text=this.state.text;
        id=DateTime.Now }]
        this.setState({ items=nextItems; text="" })
    member this.render() =
        R.div [] [
            R.h3 [] [
R.str "TODO"]
```

```
        R.com<TodoListView,_,_> this.state []
        R.form [OnSubmit this.handleSubmit] [
            R.input [OnChange this.onChange; Value (U2.Case1
            this.state.text)] []
            R.button [] [sprintf "Add #%i"
            (this.state.items.Length + 1) |>
    R.str]
        ]
    ]
```

Finally, we just need to mount our `TodoAppView` component in the actual HTML page using `ReactDom.render`, as shown in the following code snippet:

```
ReactDom.render(
    R.com<TodoAppView,_,_> None [],
    Browser.document.getElementById
"content")
```

Given that the code is being saved in a file named `script.fsx`, and that we have installed `fable-compiler` as explained previously, we can compile the code to JavaScript by typing the following in the command line:

```
fable script.fsx --module amd
```

 In the web page, we will load our code and the dependencies using RequireJS, a JavaScript module loader compatible with **Asynchronous Module Definition (AMD)**, which is why we will need to compile the code using the amd module format.

The preceding command snippet will generate the following `script.js` file, which we can include in our HTML:

```
<!DOCTYPE html>
<html>
  <head>
    <!-- Require.js is a tool to asynchrously load JS scripts in
runtime -->
    <script src="node_modules/requirejs/require.js"></script>
  </head>
  <body>
    <div id="content"></div>
    <script>
        // Tell Require.js where to find the dependencies
        // Paths in Require.js must always omit the .js extension
        requirejs.config({
            paths: {
```

```
                    'fable-core': 'node_modules/fable-core/umd',
                    'react': 'node_modules/react/dist/react',
                    'react-dom': 'node_modules/react-dom/dist/react-dom'
            }
        });
        // Now we load our custom script
        requirejs(["script"]);
    </script>
  </body>
</html>
```

We can simply install the dependencies using npm. We will cover the process in more detail in the next chapter, but for now, you just need to type the following piece of code in the command line from the same directory where index.html and script.js are:

```
npm init --yes
npm install fable-core react react-dom requirejs
```

 The first command (npm init) just initializes an empty package.json file, necessary to tell npm the modules must be saved in that directory.

Give it a try by opening the web page with a browser, and you will see that with very little code, we have built a simple but interactive to-do list.

Summary

In this chapter, we have reviewed some of the most common tools for web development with F#. We have briefly seen how web view controllers can be written using ASP.NET Web API 2, a framework designed by Microsoft for C#, but that can be easily adapted to F# thanks to its conciseness.

Then, you learned in more detail about Suave, a very popular web server in the F# community, that is specifically designed to make the most of the functional (such as expressiveness and composability) and asynchronous features of the language.

However, F# is not limited to the backend (server side). WebSharper gives you a full set of tools to write both your server and client code in F#, and takes advantage of the type safety the language provides. Also, Fable is a lightweight F# to JavaScript compiler that gives us more flexibility when we need to stay closer to the JavaScript ecosystem.

In the next chapter, we will learn more about Fable and how it can be used not only to write the frontend (client side) of our web apps but also for full desktop applications thanks to the GitHub Electron toolkit.

8
Application Development in F#

One of the most recurrent sentences of the F# advocates is that F# is not only for data science. However, until recently it was difficult to write a full application, including the **graphical user interface (GUI)**, using only F#. Besides being restricted to Windows platforms, F# support has been lagging behind C# for many years. As we will soon see, this situation has happily changed thanks to Fable and GitHub Electron, which allows us to easily create cross-platform apps entirely written in F#. Moreover, Xamarin also has a long story of F# support for mobile apps in Android and iOS.

In this chapter, we will cover the following topics:

- What is the GitHub Electron project, and how can we use it to write cross-platform desktop applications, such as OS X, Linux, and Windows, reusing our web technology's knowledge?
- Microsoft has stated it will support the development of Universal Windows Platform applications in F#. However, this is still not complete at the time of writing, so it won't be discussed in this chapter.

GitHub Electron

Electron is a project developed by GitHub, originally created for its enhanced text editor, Atom, and later rebranded and open sourced in a tool of its own so it can be used by other projects as well. Electron allows developers to build cross-platform desktop apps using web technologies such as JavaScript, HTML, and CSS.

It manages to do that by packing the following three main components:

- **Node:** This is a runtime designed to build servers in JavaScript with an event-driven, non-blocking I/O model. However, its extensive API has made it very popular among web programmers to create development tools, and Node's npm has become the largest ecosystem of open source libraries in the world.

 You will also need Node for the development of Electron apps, so if you don't have it installed in your system, you can download it from `https ://nodejs.org`.

- **Chromium**: This is an open source web browser from which Google Chrome draws its source. It shares many features with the popular Chrome browser, which means that if you're used to Chrome debugging tools, you can also use them when developing desktop apps.
- **V8**: This is a JavaScript engine developed by Google, and generally recognized as the most efficient JavaScript runtime. It's actually used by both Node and Chromium to optimize and compile JavaScript to machine code in order to get performance levels beyond a scripting language.

You may think that using HTML will be too slow for desktop application standards. However, Electron is a mature project and has proven performant enough to be used in several of the most popular desktop apps, such as Slack and Visual Studio Code. Moreover, the advantage of easily writing a cross-platform app reusing your knowledge from web development is too great to be ignored.

Still, the desktop and the web are two different environments, and there are a few concepts that we need for a better understanding of app development with Electron. First, we must know about the two kinds of processes Electron runs, which are as follows:

- **Main process**: This is the process that starts the app and manages the window, or windows, that display the GUI. There is only one main process running per app.
- **Renderer process**: This Electron spawns one specific process per web page displayed, which means that there can be multiple renderer processes running at the same time. Instead of tabs, as in the browser, Electron opens each web page in a different desktop window, aptly called `BrowserWindow`. The renderer process shares the life cycle of the window it belongs to, so whenever the window is closed, the process is terminated too.

You may feel tempted to think of the main and renderer processes as your server and client code from the web apps. This comparison can be useful in some ways, but you must also understand that Electron's `BrowserWindow` is not sandboxed and, through Node APIs, it gives access to operating system resources, which makes it more powerful than a simple web app, but at the same time, requires more care from the developer.

Another difference between the main and renderer process is that the later is not allowed to call native GUI-related APIs, as this is prone to leak resources and must be done from the main process. Later, we will see how the main and renderer processes can communicate. Likewise, each `BrowserWindow` class runs its own isolated renderer process, and specific ways of communication must be used to share data between them.

When developing Electron apps, we will use some common tools in modern JavaScript development. Now we will quickly overview what these tools are and their main features.

npm

As mentioned earlier, npm is Node's package manager, and it comes bundled in the Node installer. It is mainly used to both acquire dependencies and to publish our app in the npm register. However, its flexibility has extended npm to other uses as well: it can run development scripts, install commands in the global `PATH`, and acquire files other than JavaScript.

All the npm-related configuration is done in a single `package.json` file located in the root directory of our app. As the JSON format is human readable, it is easy to edit this file manually, but npm also offers several commands to update it automatically. In the following sections, you will learn how to create and update this file step by step for our examples.

The npm tool follows semantic versioning and uses the `commonjs` module system to retrieve files from within the JavaScript code.

webpack

Although not strictly necessary to develop Electron or web apps, it is usual that `node_modules`, the directory where npm installs dependencies, quickly grows to a size that is prohibitive to be deployed with our app, so it has become common to use bundlers that pack only the code that is needed to run the app in one single file. Two popular such bundlers are **Browserify** and **webpack**.

The latter, although it requires a somewhat more complicated configuration, is more versatile, and is the one we will be using in our examples.

The configuration of webpack parameters can be passed through its CLI, but it's more common to put them in a `webpack.config.js` file. Unlike `package.json`, this is an actual JavaScript that can contain any arbitrary code and access Node APIs.

So far, we have only talked about HTML, CSS, and JavaScript. F# hasn't come into play yet. Remember in the previous chapter we introduced Fable, a F# to JavaScript compiler that is not compromised with any specific framework or architecture. This means Fable is flexible enough to seamlessly integrate with the Electron app development workflow.

The best way to learn how to create Electron apps with Fable is to build a hello world sample. We will add the necessary files step by step, but the final structure, which will be similar to that used in other examples, will look like this:

```
/
├ src/
    ├ renderer.fsx
    └ main.fsx
├ app/
    ├ js/
    └ index.html
├ temp/
├ node_modules/
├ weppack.config.js
├ package.json
└ fableconfig.json
```

Following is the description of all the folders in an Electron app:

- `src`: This is the directory containing our F# source files. For this simple example, we won't use an F# project file (`.fsproj`), but we will use standalone `.fsx` scripts instead–one for the main process and another for the renderer process.
- `app`: This is the directory that will contain the final files used by our app. For this occasion, we just have a single HTML file and a `js` directory where we will put the final compiled and bundled JavaScript code files.

- `temp`: This is an automatically generated temporary directory where Fable will put the compiled JavaScript files so webpack can read and bundle them together with its dependencies.
- `node_modules`: This is also automatically generated, and it is where npm will install the dependencies specified in `package.json`.
- `webpack.config.js`: This is the first of our three main configuration files, and it is used to pass configuration options to webpack. As it is a normal JavaScript code, we can also add some other operations that we want to execute when calling webpack, such as copying files from one folder to another.
- `package.json`: This is, as mentioned in the preceding section, a plain JSON file containing npm-related options such as dependencies, build scripts, package name, and so on. It is easy to edit it manually, but you will learn how to do most updates using npm commands.
- `fableconfig.json`: This is our last config file, and it is also in a JSON format. It is mainly a convenient way to store the compiler arguments that we want to pass to Fable, but it may also contain some specific options that are not understood by the CLI, such as scripts.

If you are using a Git repository, remember to add `node_modules` and `temp` to `.gitignore` in order to prevent pollution of the repository.

As you can see, our basic structure contains multiple files of different formats and no solution (`.sln`) or project (`.fsproj`) files that are used to determine the structure in Visual Studio. Because of this, for our example, it is recommended to use an IDE that just identifies projects by folder, such as Visual Studio Code with the Ionide extension to edit F# files.

In any case, what we see in the preceding code structure is what the final file structure should look like. We will start with an empty folder and file, one by one, to learn all the steps involved in the development process. That said, create an empty directory for our hello world app, open a terminal window there, and type the following to create the `package.json` file:

```
npm init
```

 The npm tool will ask you for some information about your app, such as name, version, and author. If you just want to use the default values, add the `--yes` option.

Now, let's add our dependencies. For this example, we will just need `fable-core`, which must be added to all Fable projects. Note that by adding `--save`, besides downloading the files to the `node_modules` folder, npm also adds it to the list of dependencies in `package.json`:

```
npm install --save fable-core
```

The npm tool also has the concept of development dependencies. For this example, it is not actually necessary to make the distinction, but if we were to distribute our app through npm, normal dependencies will be installed for all consumers of the package, while development dependencies will only be installed on the development machine; so, it is good to form a habit of installing them separately:

```
npm install --save-dev electron-prebuilt webpack source-map-loader fable-import-electron
```

 Note that the `--save-dev` option tells npm to save the modules as `devDependencies` in `package.json`. Also, note that you can install different packages at the same time by separating them with a space.

Let's review the packages we just installed:

- `electron-prebuilt`: This is a precompiled version of Electron that will run our app. It can be installed globally, but adding it as a local dependency makes it easier to build the app in different machines and manage specific Electron versions for each app.
- `webpack`: This is the development tool that we will use to bundle our JavaScript files. As with `electron-prebuilt`, it can also be installed globally.
- `source-map-loader`: This is a webpack plugin that loads JavaScript source maps. It is necessary to include the source maps generated by Fable in the final bundle and still be able to debug the original F# code after all the transformations.
- `fable-import-electron`: We will see later that Fable can interact with JavaScript both statically and dynamically. For the latter, we must define **foreign function interfaces** (**FFI**) for the JavaScript objects we want to interact with. The `Fable.Core` library already includes definitions for native JavaScript, browser, and Node APIs, and there are some packages available for common JavaScript libraries generated from TypeScript definition files, which can be found in npm with the `fable-import-` prefix. In this case, we are downloading the definitions of Electron APIs.

To complete our `package.json`, we will just need to add the very simple script that will start our app. This cannot be done from the command line, so use the IDE of your choice to edit the JSON file. You should find a `scripts` field in the root object (just add it if you don't), which should contain a nested object where you must add the following key-value pair:

```
"start": "electron app/js/main.js"
```

Now your `package.json` should look something similar to the following listing:

```
{
  "name": "my-app",
  "version": "1.0.0",
  "description": "",
  "main": "index.js",
  "scripts": {
    "start": "electron app/js/main.js",
    "test": "echo "Error: no test specified" && exit 1"
  },
  "keywords": [],
  "author": "",
  "license": "ISC",
  "dependencies": {
    "fable-core": "^0.1.12"
  },
  "devDependencies": {
    "electron-prebuilt": "^1.2.7",
    "fable-import-electron": "0.0.5",
    "source-map-loader": "^0.1.5",
    "webpack": "^1.13.1"
  }
}
```

There is still some configuration missing, but let's skip the boilerplate for now and jump directly to the code! Create an `src` subdirectory and a `main.fsx` file within it, edit it with an F# IDE, and let's start typing the following code:

```
#r "../node_modules/fable-core/Fable.Core.dll"
#load "../node_modules/fable-import-electron/Fable.Import.Electron.fs"
open Fable.Core
open Fable.Import
open Fable.Import.Electron

// Keep a global reference of the window object.
// If you don't, the window will be closed automatically
// when the JavaScript object is garbage collected.
let mutable mainWindow: BrowserWindow option = Option.None
```

As with most Fable scripts, we will start by adding a reference to `Fable.Core.dll`, and in this case, also loading the file containing the type definitions for Electron, both of which are located in the `node_modules` folder. After that, we will open the modules that we will use, and we will create a global reference for our main window. Using global mutable variables is not a good practice in functional programming in most cases but, as stated in the comment, it is necessary here to prevent the JavaScript object as it gets garbage collected and the window is closed.

 When we say global here, we talk about the global scope within the module. Fable compiles code using JavaScript modules, which prevent global name pollution.

Next, we will write the method to create the main window, as follows:

```
let createMainWindow () =
    let options = createEmpty<BrowserWindowOptions>
    options.width <- Some 800.
    options.height <- Some 600.
    let window = electron.BrowserWindow.Create(options)

    // Load the index.html of the app.
    window.loadURL("file://" + Node.__dirname + "/../index.html");

    #if DEBUG
    fs.watch(Node.__dirname + "/renderer.js", fun _ ->
        window.webContents.reloadIgnoringCache() |> ignore
    ) |> ignore
    #endif

    // Emitted when the window is closed.
    window.on("closed", unbox(fun () ->
        // Dereference the window object. Usually
        // you would store windows in an array.
        // If your app supports multi windows,
        // this is the time when you should delete
        // the corresponding element.
        mainWindow <- Option.None
    )) |> ignore

    mainWindow <- Some window
```

We will use the `createEmpty` method from `Fable.Core` to create the options that will be passed to `electron.BrowserWindow.Create`. The `createEmpty` method actually just creates an empty JavaScript object but assigns an interface that helps us explore its fields using the IDE autocompletion. Note that all members in `BrowserWindowOptions` have the option type; this is the way Fable translate the optional members of a JavaScript object.

After creating the window, we will load our `index.html` with a file path URL. The `Node.__dirname` parameter will be replaced by the directory where the JavaScript script is found. Remember that we intend to put the final `main.js`, in the `app/js` directory, and thus we will have to navigate one directory back to find `index.html`.

Let's skip the code within the `#if DEBUG` compiler directive for now. Later, we will use it to refresh the window whenever the renderer script changes. Notice also that this code will actually be compiled to JavaScript if we pass the `DEBUG` symbol to the Fable compiler.

There is no other work left to be done except attaching a callback to the close event of the window and assigning our window to `mainWindow`. In the callback, we will actually do the opposite and dereference the global `mainWindow` variable (by assigning `Option.None` to it, which translates as JavaScript to `null`) so it can be garbage collected. Note that the signature of `window.on` expects `JS.Function`; this is because `Fable.Import` definitions are usually translated automatically from TypeScript and there can be imperfections sometimes. In this case, we know our callback will translate to a JavaScript function so we can safely cast it using `unbox`.

We will finish by adding listeners to some other events in the `Electron.App` object:

```
// This method will be called when Electron has finished
// initialization and is ready to create browser windows.
electron.app.on("ready", unbox createMainWindow)

// Quit when all windows are closed.
electron.app.on("window-all-closed", unbox(fun () ->
    // On OS X it is common for applications and their menu bar
    // to stay active until the user quits explicitly with Cmd + Q
    if Node.``process``.platform <> "darwin" then
        electron.app.quit()
))
electron.app.on("activate", unbox(fun () ->
    // On OS X it's common to re-create a window in the app when the
    // dock icon is clicked and there are no other windows open.
    if mainWindow.IsNone then
        createMainWindow()
))
```

The script for the main process is done; we will just need another one for the renderer process, which we will aptly name renderer.fsx:

```
#r "../node_modules/fable-core/Fable.Core.dll"

open Fable.Import
let body = Browser.document.getElementsByTagName_h1().[0]
body.textContent <- "Hello World!"
```

As this is a hello world example, the code is actually very simple; we will use the Browser DOM API to find the first <h1> tag and write "Hello World!". However, don't worry; we won't be manipulating the DOM directly in the next examples.

We are done with the F# code, so let's get back to our configuration files. First, let's set webpack up. Create a file named webpack.config.js (this is the file that webpack loads by default) in the root directory of your app and type the following:

```
module.exports = {
  entry: {
    main: "./temp/src/main",
    renderer: "./temp/src/renderer"
  },
  output: {
    filename: "[name].js",
    path: "./app/js",
    libraryTarget: "commonjs2"
  },
  target: "node",
  node: {
    __dirname: false,
    __filename: false
  },
  externals: {
    electron: true
  },
  devtool: "source-map",
  module: {
    preLoaders: [{
      loader: "source-map-loader",
      exclude: /node_modules/,
      test: /\.js$/
    }]
  }
};
```

The webpack is a very versatile tool, which also means that its configuration files can look a bit daunting. The first thing we should notice is that, unlike the other configuration files, this is an actual JavaScript that can execute any arbitrary code, and also requires modules and call Node APIs. In fact, we will expose our configuration object (a plain JavaScript object) by assigning it to `module.exports`.

The webpack has multiple options and it is not possible to list them here (if necessary, please check its comprehensive website at `https://webpack.github.io/`), but we will briefly overview the options used in our configuration file:

- `entry`: This is the script file that determines the dependency graph. As the scripts for the main and renderer processes must be isolated, here we are using multiple entries to generate two independent bundles.
- `output`: This defines three fields, namely: `path`, where we want to put the generated bundles; `filename`, how we name the bundle (note that we will use the macro `[name]`, which will be replaced by the name of each entry); and `libraryTarget`, which defines the module system used for our exports and the external modules, set to `commonjs2`, which is the one compatible with Electron.
- `target`: Even if webpack allows `electron` as a target, we will use `"node"` in order to be able to set specific `node` options.
- `node`: For some mysterious reasons, webpack replaces Node's `__dirname` and `__filename` macros in the generated bundle. To prevent this rather unintuitive behavior, we must add this field and set the value of both macros to `false`, which basically means don't touch them. This only works when `target` is set to `node`.
- `externals`: We must tell webpack that `electron` is an external value and shouldn't be included in the bundle. As we set `output.libraryTarget` to `commonjs2`, all `electron` import references will be replaced by `require` calls.
- `devtool`: This determines the way webpack packs and runs bundled modules, and it affects the debugging experience and build speed. In our case, we will choose `"source-map"` because it's the only one compatible with the `source-map-loader` package.

- `module`: This is normally used to include the loaders we want to use. In webpack, loaders are a kind of plugin that transforms different types of files loaded into the final bundle. This is how webpack loader can include CSS within your JavaScript bundle, for example. The webpack loaders are a broad topic, and you must check the website if you want to go deeper. Here, we will only need to use the `source-map-loader` package as `preLoader`. This makes webpack load not only the JS generated by Fable, but also the source maps, so we can still debug the original F# code. Note that loaders also have options of its own; here, we will pass two regular expressions to use the loader for all files with the `.js` extension (`test`), but at the same time, ignoring anything in the `node_modules` folder (`exclude`).

Only the configuration file for Fable remains. Hopefully, this one is a bit shorter. Create a file named `fableconfig.json` and type the following code:

```
{
    "projFile": ["src/main.fsx", "src/renderer.fsx"],
    "coreLib": "fable-core/umd",
    "outDir": "temp",
    "module": "commonjs",
    "sourceMaps": true,
    "scripts": {
        "prebuild": "npm install",
        "postbuild": "node node_modules/webpack/bin/webpack"
    }
}
```

This configuration is much simpler and just tells Fable the following: load `src/main.fsx` and `src/renderer.fsx` as project files (it is necessary to include both because there are no links between each other in the code) and put the compiled JavaScript code in the `temp` folder, where they will be found by webpack; also, use `commonjs` modules, the UMD distribution of fable-core, which is compatible with `commonjs` modules, and generate source maps. We are also adding a `scripts` object, which is similar to the option of the same name in `package.json`, though a bit less powerful; for example, Fable cannot find binaries automatically in `node_modules`). At the time of writing, Fable just supports three types of scripts: `prebuild`, which will run before the F# to JavaScript compilation; `postbuild`, which runs after each compilation, even when using the `--watch` option; and `postbuild-once`, which we will see later. Here, we will make sure the dependencies are installed by running `npm install` at the beginning, and we will call webpack right after the JavaScript files are generated.

We are almost ready to run our app; the only thing left is the HTML for our web page. Create an `app` directory, and within it, an `index.html` file with the following code:

```html
<!DOCTYPE html>
<html>
  <head>
    <meta charset="UTF-8">
    <title>Hello World!</title>
  </head>
  <body>
    <h1></h1>
    <script src="js/renderer.js"></script>
  </body>

</html>
```

The output for the preceding code would look similar to the following screenshot:

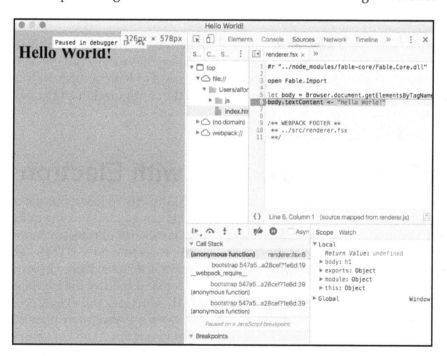

Now open a terminal window in the root directory of the app and type the following:

```
fable
```

If Fable is not installed in your system, you can install or update it with `npm install --global fable-compiler`; in OS X, you may need to use `sudo`).

Fable will read the compilation options directly from `fableconfig.json`, so we do not need to pass any extra arguments. After F# to JavaScript compilation has finished, type the following:

```
npm start
```

This, as we saw in the preceding code snippet, just calls the `"start"` script in `package.json`, which is `"electron bundle/js/main.js"`. If everything goes right, an app window will open with the message **Hello World!**. You can see this is an actual browser embedded in the app by opening the debugger tools (with the shortcut *Ctrl+Alt+I*, or *Cmd+Alt+I* on OS X), which correspond to the same thing you can see on the Google Chrome browser.

It may seem that this is not very impressive for all the configuration we had to do, but the good news is that we can reuse most of the configuration files for the other examples we will see. We went through everything step by step instead of having the boilerplate set up for us in order to learn what is the role of each file in the configuration and make it easier to edit them when needed.

Using React components with Electron

In the hello world example, we manipulated the DOM directly to insert our message. However, anybody who has done web apps knows this can quickly become quite complicated. Because of this, there are many popular JavaScript libraries or frameworks that abstract DOM manipulation and provides us with tools to render HTML views on the client side in an easy and efficient way. One such library is React, which we saw in the previous chapter. Among other advantages of React is that it follows the components architecture, so our views encapsulate the logic, HTML structure, and even CSS styles and can easily be reused in multiple apps. Thanks to this, there are also many open source libraries containing React components that we can use in our apps and customize when necessary through the React `props` system. For this occasion, we will test the `material-ui` library, which provides components following the Material UI style guidelines created by Google for the Android operating system but that, thanks to its beautiful animations and responsiveness to different screen sizes, can be successfully applied to other environments as well.

Remember all the configuration files that we had to write for the previous example? Luckily, we can reuse most of them, so we will start by copying the directory containing our hello world app and renaming it. However, we will need to install the dependencies for the new example. Open a terminal window in the directory of the new app and type the following piece of code:

```
npm install --save react react-dom react-tap-event-plugin material-ui
npm install --save-dev fable-react
npm install
```

As you can see, we are installing the React and Material UI libraries, plus the React tap event plugin, and also the React definitions that are available for Fable (remember we installed this as a development dependency). Finally, we will run `npm install` to download the other packages in `package.json`, which are the same as for the hello world example.

We will be reusing the same `files.fsx` and `main.fsx` scripts, so we will only need to edit `renderer.fsx`. Start by typing the following code:

```
#r "../node_modules/fable-core/Fable.Core.dll"
#r "../node_modules/fable-react/Fable.React.dll"

open System
open Fable.Core
open Fable.Import
open Fable.Import.Browser
open Fable.Helpers.React.Props

module R = Fable.Helpers.React
type RCom = React.ComponentClass<obj>

let deepOrange500 = importMember<string> "material-ui/styles/colors"
let RaisedButton = importDefault<RCom> "material-ui/RaisedButton"
let Dialog = importDefault<RCom> "material-ui/Dialog"
let FlatButton = importDefault<RCom> "material-ui/FlatButton"
let MuiThemeProvider =
    importDefault<RCom> "material-ui/styles/MuiThemeProvider"
let getMuiTheme =
    importDefault<obj->obj> "material-ui/styles/getMuiTheme"

let inline (~%) x = createObj x
let inline (=>) x y = x ==> y
```

As usual, we will add the necessary references on top of the script. Note that the `fable-react` package, besides the React definitions, also contains helpers to make React development more idiomatic in F#.

After that, we will open the necessary namespaces and define a couple of aliases for a module (`Fable.Helpers.React`) and a type (`React.ComponentClass<obj>`) to save some typing and make our code cleaner.

The next lines of the code are more interesting. We have already mentioned that Fable organizes the generated code using JavaScript modules. By default, it uses ES2015 modules, which can be later converted to the module system defined in `fableconfig.json` or as a compiler argument. Most of the time, Fable automatically generates the necessary imports and exports, but for the situations when we need to define them explicitly (for example, when using JavaScript libraries without definitions as here with Material UI), `Fable.Core` provides three helper methods, which translate to JavaScript as follows:

```
let deepOrange500 = importMember<string> "material-ui/styles/colors"
// import { deepOrange500 } from "material-ui/styles/colors"

let RaisedButton = importDefault<RCom> "material-ui/RaisedButton"
// import RaisedButton from "material-ui/RaisedButton"

let styles = importAll<obj> "material-ui/styles"
// import * as styles from "material-ui/styles"
```

You can learn more about ES2015 modules in the **Mozilla Developer Network (MDN)** (htt ps://developer.mozilla.org/en/docs/web/javascript/reference/statements/impor t).

As we will be using a bit of dynamic programming in this example, in the last two lines of the preceding code snippet, we will define some operators to create JavaScript object literals with a syntax which is a bit terser. We will use `inline` so these operators are actually removed from the generated code.

We will continue editing `renderer.fsx` by defining our React component, as follows:

```
let muiTheme =
    %["palette" =>
        %["accent1Color" => deepOrange500]]
    |> getMuiTheme

type MainState = { isOpen: bool; secret: string }

type Main(props) as this =
    inherit React.Component<obj,MainState>(props)
    do this.state <- {isOpen=false; secret=""}

    member this.handleRequestClose() =
        this.setState({isOpen=false; secret=""})
```

```
member this.handleTouchTap () =
    this.setState({isOpen=true; secret="1-2-3-4-5"})

member this.render () =
    let standardActions =
        R.from FlatButton
            %["label" => "Ok"
              "primary" => true
              "onTouchTap" => this.handleRequestClose] []
    R.from MuiThemeProvider
        %["muiTheme" => muiTheme] [
            R.div [Style [TextAlign "center"
                          PaddingTop 200]] [
                R.from Dialog
                    %["open" => this.state.isOpen
                      "title" => "Super Secret Password"
                      "actions" => standardActions
                      "onRequestClose" =>
                          this.handleRequestClose]
                    [R.str this.state.secret]
                R.h1 [] [R.str "Material-UI"]
                R.h2 [] [R.str "example project"]
                R.from RaisedButton
                    %["label" => "Super Secret Password"
                      "secondary" => true
                      "onTouchTap" => this.handleTouchTap] []
            ]
        ]
```

Before defining our React component, we will define the type of the component state (a simple F# record) and build the Material UI theme that we will use. Note how we used the operators defined earlier to build the JavaScript object literal. JavaScript object literals are very important to interact with libraries and pass them options, and Fable allows you to define them in a very simple way. The first lines of the code in the preceding snippet will translate to the following straightforward JavaScript:

```
var muiTheme = getMuiTheme({
    palette: { accent1Color: deepOrange500 }
});
```

The usual way to define custom React components with Fable is ES2015 (also known as ES6) classes, and the way to do it in Fable is almost identical to how it would be done in JavaScript. For more information about it, check out at https://facebook.github.io/react/docs/reusable-components.html#es6-classes.

The most important method this class must implement is `render`, which is called every time the view must be rendered on screen. The `render` method returns the smaller components from which our custom component is made. To express these components, React apps often use a declarative language developed by Facebook called JSX. However, thanks to F# expressiveness, we can create a similar DSL with no foreign syntax. This DSL is included in the `Fable.Helpers.React` namespace, for which we have defined the `R` alias, and includes five main kinds of function, which are as follows:

- `R.com`: This is used for custom components. It is a generic function, and for the first generic argument, we will need to specify the type the component is made from, for example, `R.com<Main,_,_>`.
- `R.from`: This is also for custom components, but instead of a type, we will directly pass an object. It is often used with components that we have imported from an external library. In this example, we will use it to declare Material UI components.
- `R.fn`: We will not see them in this example, but it is also possible to define React components with simple functions; basically, reducing the component to the `render` method. This helper builds a component from a function with the `'Props -> #React.ReactElement<obj>` signature.
- `DOM tags`: This is like `R.div`, `R.h1`, `R.a`, and so on.
- `SVG tags`: This is like `R.circle`, `R.ellipse`, `R.line`, and so on.

All these functions have a very similar signature—they all accept a `props` object and a list of child components. Before going any further, it is important to understand the distinction that React makes between `props` and `state` object:

- `props`: This is short for properties—an object to describe the configuration of the component. The biggest difference with the `state` is that `props` are immutable and are received in the constructor.
- `state`: Some components need to keep track of a mutable state. This `state` is private; it can only be modified by the component itself. The initial state is set in the constructor, and it can later be modified using `setState`, which causes the component to be rendered again. It is advisable to try to reduce stateful components to a minimum.

There are two common techniques to manage `state` and `props`: firstly, the `state` object (or part of it) of a component becomes the `props` object of its children, and second, the parent passes callbacks to its children through the `props` object to modify its own `state`.

Our `Main` component inherits from `React.Component` and uses the `obj` type for its `props` (actually, this component ignores the `props` object) and `MainState` for its `state`. You can see how we set the initial state with a simple assignment in the constructor. From that moment on, we will need to use `setState` to trigger new renderings with state changes.

As expected, the elaborated method is `render`. The child components of `Main` have the following structure:

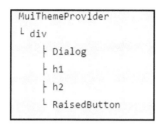

Note that the root component is a `MuiThemeProvider` component to determine the style of our app. This component must have a single child, which in this case is an HTML `div` element, and can contain other components on its own; in our example, `Dialog`, `h1` and `h2` HTML tags, and `RaisedButton`. We will see in the following sections how the Material UI `Dialog` starts hiding, and to open it, we will only need to pass a `props` object with an `open: true` field, which is actually part of the `Main` state. Also, as it is common with React components, we will pass a callback through the `props` object to modify `Main` state when the user closes the dialog.

Another thing we must note is that React accepts plain strings as component children. However, the signature of Fable helpers only accepts a list of `ReactElement<obj>`. To overcome this, we will use `unbox` to ignore the compiler type check in this case.

We will only need to add two more lines to finish `renderer.fsx`, which are as follows:

```
(importDefault "react-tap-event-plugin")()
ReactDom.render(
    R.com<Main,_,_> None [],
    document.getElementById("app")
)
```

Material UI needs the `react-tap-event-plugin` package, so before rendering our component, we will import and immediately apply it. After that, we will call the `ReactDom.render` method to mount our `Main` component on the element in our HTML document with the `"app"` ID.

We are done with the F# code. We only need to adjust our `index.html`, file, and for this occasion, we will also add some CSS. First, edit `app/index.html` so it looks something like this:

```
<!doctype html>
<html lang="en" data-framework="react">
    <head>
        <meta charset="utf-8">
        <title>Fable + Material UI</title>
        <link rel="stylesheet" type="text/css" href="css/styles.css">
    </head>
    <body>
        <div id="app"></div>
        <script src="js/renderer.js"></script>
    </body>
</html>
```

As usual, the HTML code in React apps is quite simple because most of the view code is defined directly in JavaScript; in our case, F#. Now we will create a `css` folder within `app` and put a `styles.css` file in it, as follows:

```
@font-face {
    font-family: Roboto;
    src: url(Roboto-Medium.ttf);
}
html {
    font-family: 'Roboto', sans-serif;
}
body {
    font-size: 13px;
    line-height: 20px;
}
```

The CSS code is also very simple, and its main task is to load the `Roboto` font. This is the font the Material UI components work best with, and it can be downloaded from `https://f onts.google.com`. After downloading the ZIP file, extract the `Roboto-Medium.ttf` file and put it next to `app/css/styles.css`. With that, we are ready to test our app. Like we did earlier, open a terminal window in the directory where `fableconfig.json` is and type the following:

```
fable
```

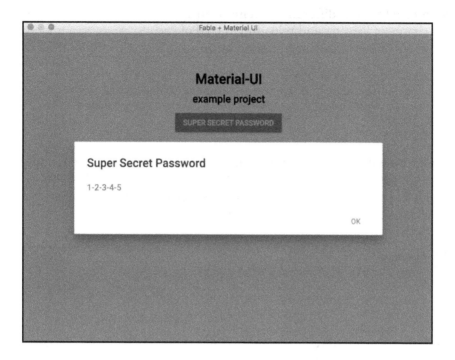

npm start

This is another simple example, but thanks to Material UI with very few lines of code, we will have components such as a modal dialog with nice animations. The library contains many more components that you can easily integrate into your app, the same way we have done in the sample. You can find a full list at `http://www.material-ui.com/#/components`
.

Automatic refresh on code changes

One of the reasons web UI development has become so popular and hybrid apps are also taking over mobile and desktop is its development workflow. As neither JavaScript, HTML, nor CSS are compiled languages, the only thing a developer had to do to see changes in their code reflected on screen was to refresh the browser. Now, there are even tools to omit this step so that developers can keep working on their IDEs and see the browser refresh itself. Using F#, we had to add an extra compilation step, but thanks to Fable's `--watch` option, it is still possible to get very close to this experience.

The way to refresh the UI is different in an Electron app. As you may guess, the main process is in charge of loading and reloading the UI of each `BrowserWindow`. Remember the lines we wrote in `main.fsx`, surrounded by an `#IF DEBUG` compiler directive?

```
#if DEBUG
Node.fs.watch(Node.__dirname + "/renderer.js", fun _ ->
    window.webContents.reloadIgnoringCache() |> ignore
) |> ignore
#endif
```

Now their purpose will become clear. They just watch for changes in the renderer script and, when this happens, reload the contents of the `BrowserWindow` class. But we have to define the `DEBUG` symbol so that these lines are actually compiled to JavaScript. For that, we will have to change `fableconfig.json` a bit:

```
{
    "module": "commonjs",
    "projFile": ["src/main.fsx", "src/renderer.fsx"],
    "coreLib": "fable-core/umd",
    "outDir": "temp",
    "scripts": {
        "prebuild": "npm install",
        "postbuild": "node node_modules/webpack/bin/webpack"
    },
    "targets": {
        "debug": {
            "watch": true,
            "symbols": ["DEBUG"],
            "sourceMaps": true,
            "scripts": {
                "postbuild": "",
                "postbuild-once": "node
node_modules/webpack/bin/webpack --watch"
            }
        }
    }
}
```

What we have done here is just add the `"targets"` field. Like `"scripts"`, `"targets"` contain another object whose keys are the names of the compilation target, and the values are the options that will overwrite or add to the default options. We will call Fable again, but this time, by activating the `"debug"` target, as follows:

```
fable --target debug
```

The `fable -d` command is short for `fable --target debug`, and `fable -p` becomes `fable --target production`.

You will notice that this time, the process doesn't exist because it remains watching for changes in our source files. Because of this, we must open a new terminal window to run `npm start`. After doing that, try to make any (valid) code change (for example, modify the content of the `h1` and `h2` tags or the label of the button) and save the file. You will see that a new, and much faster compilation is triggered, and after a few seconds, the app window is reloaded to reflect the new code.

In order to also take advantage of the webpack `watch` mode, in the `"debug"` target, we will clear the `postbuild` script and use `postbuild-once`, which will only run once after the first compilation to start webpack in `watch` mode.

Using Node APIs from the renderer process

Earlier, we said that one of the important differences of Electron windows with the browser is the accessibility to Node APIs, so it is time to quickly check this feature–instead of hard coding our super secret password, let's read it from a file. Create a `data` folder within `app`, add a `secret.txt` file to it, and put whatever you want in there–if I told you what to write, it wouldn't be a secret. In `renderer.fsx`, add the following line to the other `open` statements:

```
open Fable.Import.Node
```

Now we will edit the `handleTouchTap` method of our `Main` component so it looks like this:

```
member this.handleTouchTap() =
    fs.readFile(__dirname + "/data/secret.txt", fun err buffer ->
        if (box err) <> null then
            failwith "Couldn't read file"
        this.setState({isOpen=true; secret=string buffer}))
```

Note that `__dirname` is not replaced by the directory where the JavaScript is (`/app/js`) but by the one containing the HTML of the web page.

If Fable is still watching, you will only have to click the **SUPER SECRET PASSWORD** button in your app to verify that now the data is being read from your filesystem. The same way as you can read, you can also save files, move them, and so on. All of this makes Electron apps more powerful than simple web apps, but it also means that you must put extra care when using these APIs to prevent damaging the user system.

Summary

In this chapter, you learned how to create cross-platform desktop applications in F# using Fable and GitHub Electron. Moreover, you can recycle your knowledge of web technologies when building applications with Electron, making it much easier to share code between different versions of your app.

Although we could not cover them here, there are also many more possibilities to write applications in F#. With Fable, it is also possible to use React Native to create mobile apps that use native components, and using the open source Xamarin tools, you can write a single code base that has access to the full .NET framework and compiles to native code both on iOS and Android. And obviously, it is possible to create desktop applications for Windows using the well-known `Windows.Forms` and **Windows Presentation Foundation** (**WPF**) framework, with support for native universal apps that can run on multiple Windows platforms coming soon, such as Windows 10, Xbox, and so on.

In the next chapter, you will learn about the different ways of automating code testing in F# to ensure the robustness of your software.

9
Testing in F#

Enthusiasts of typed functional languages tend to say that the only errors you need to care about are compilation errors. That would indeed be the ideal situation, but even a compiler as advanced as F#'s cannot detect all errors; it is still necessary to test your code. For many years now, programmers have learned to automate these tests to avoid the time-consuming process of manual testing. There are many great tools for automated testing for all popular languages, and F# is no exception. In this chapter, we will overview several techniques from the widely used unit tests to the more advanced property-based testing.

In this chapter, we will cover the following topics:

- How to write unit tests in F# with the popular NUnit tool, and the advantages the language offers for this. We will also see how to easily run tests in our builds with **FAKE** to make sure we haven't introduced regression bugs with our changes.
- Property-based testing with **FsCheck** is a more robust way to verify our program. Instead of manually setting the parameters when testing our functions, as with unit tests (which entails the risk of missing some cases), we can define some properties that our program must fulfill, and FsCheck will randomly generate hundreds of values to feed our functions and make sure nothing produces unexpected results. This kind of testing takes more time to set up, but it always pays off thanks to the strong verification it provides.
- Canopy are the techniques mentioned earlier that are usually very good at testing the program logic, but for the UI, things get more complicated. So, we will finish the chapter with **Canopy**–a tool designed to make automated browser UI testing as easy as possible.

Unit testing

Unit testing is perhaps the easiest and most widely used technique to write automated tests. It consists of dividing our program into **units**, running each of these units in isolation, and then making sure that it produces the expected results. Ideally, tests should cover all units of our program so that no part of the code is left untested before deploying it to production. In functional programming, these units normally correspond to functions, and because there is no shared state, these functions can easily be tested in isolation from the rest of the program.

Unit tests with NUnit

There are several libraries that help us write unit tests for .NET. Here, we will use one of the most popular ones – NUnit. NUnit is compatible both with C# and F#, so if you have any previous development experience in C#, chances are that you already know how to use it. Writing tests with NUnit is very easy. Let's say you have a module (MyLib.fs) such as the following:

```
module MyLib

let add x y =
    x + y

let multiply x y =
    x * y

let tryDivide x y =
    if y = 0
    then None
    else Some(x / y)
```

Now we will write some tests for it in MyLibTests.fsx:

```
module MyLibTests
#r "../packages/NUnit/lib/net45/nunit.framework.dll"
#load "MyLib.fs"

open MyLib
open NUnit.Framework

[<Test>]
let ``Adding two plus two yields four``() =
    Assert.AreEqual(4, add 2 2)
```

For convenience, we are using F# `.fsx` scripts, but it will work the same way with `.fsproj` project files.

If you have used NUnit or a similar library with an OOP language such as C#, there are a couple of things that you may have noticed:

- We can use a module as a test suite instead of a static class, and we do not need `TestFixtureAttribute`
- As F# accepts spaces in the name of module functions, it's easy to use a descriptive and readable name for the tests, which will produce a nicer test report

Sometimes, we want to feed different values to the same case. This is easy in NUnit with `TestCaseAttribute`:

```
[<TestCase(2, 2, 4)>]
[<TestCase(2, 3, 5)>]
[<TestCase(5, 5, 10)>]
let ``Adding integers`` (x: int, y: int, result: int) =
    Assert.AreEqual(result, add x y)
```

On executing the preceding code, `Adding integers` will be run three times. Note that this time the test method accepts three arguments, which correspond to the values passed to each of the instances of `TestCaseAttribute`. The gain is not clear in this simple example, but when we have a more complex test logic, this is a very convenient way to reuse a test. Besides that, NUnit generates a different test for each `TestCaseAttribute`, making it easier to spot which values are causing the problem if we get an error in the test report.

Another way to write the previous example, with maybe clearer semantics, is the following:

```
[<TestCase(2, 2, ExpectedResult=4)>]
[<TestCase(2, 3, ExpectedResult=5)>]
[<TestCase(5, 5, ExpectedResult=10)>]
let ``Adding integers`` (x: int, y: int) =
    add x y
```

In the preceding code, we indicate to `TestCaseAttribute` which value is the expected result, so it doesn't need to be included in the arguments, and NUnit will also generate the assertion automatically with the result of the test function.

Sometimes, we also want to automate the generation of values for our tests; this is also possible with `TestCaseSourceAttribute`:

```fsharp
[<TestCaseSource("addCases")>]
let ``Adding integers`` (x: int, y: int, result: int) =
    Assert.AreEqual(result, add x y)

let addCases = seq {
    for i in [0..2..10] do
      for j in [10..-3..-10] do
        yield [| i; j; i+j |]
}
```

`TestCaseSourceAttribute` just contains the name of a property in the same module, returning a `seq` (`IEnumerable`) of arrays matching the number and type of the parameters of the test. We will see later how the automatic generation of test values can evolve into property-based testing.

> There are more possibilities to indicate the source of the test values in `TestCaseSourceAttribute`; check the NUnit documentation for more info.

Setting up the test environment

Thanks to the use of pure functions and the absence of shared state in functional programming, it's usually very easy to tests the units of our program in isolation. However, it is still sometimes necessary to set up things before running our tests (maybe start a database or web server) and/or doing some cleanup after that. NUnit provides several useful attributes for this purpose, which are as follows:

```fsharp
[<OneTimeSetUp>]
let oneTimeSetup() =
    printfn "This setup happens only once"

[<SetUp>]
let setup() =
    printfn "This setup happens before every test"

[<TearDown>]
let cleanup() =
    printfn "This cleanup happens after every test"
```

```
[<OneTimeTearDown>]
let oneTimeCleanup () =
    printfn "This cleanup happens only once"
```

 Note that these are NUnit 3 attributes that have changed slightly from the previous versions. Please check the NUnit documentation for more information.

Mocking

In some cases, our tests must interact with external interfaces, and we just need to mock up these interfaces for the sake of the tests. F# **object expressions** are a good fit for this:

```
type ICustomer =
    abstract Name: string
    abstract HasBoughtItem: itemId: int -> bool

let createCustomer name =
    { new ICustomer with
        member __.Name = name
        member __.HasBoughtItem(_) = failwith "Not implemented" }

// Say there is a function with this signature in MyLib
// val validateCustomer: ICustomer -> bool

[<Test>]
let ``Customer names with spaces are not valid``() =
    let customer1 = createCustomer "John"
    let customer2 = createCustomer "Anne Mary"
    Assert.AreEqual(true, validateCustomer customer1)
    Assert.AreEqual(false, validateCustomer customer2)
```

When the interface is too complex to be easily implemented with an object expression, and we are only interested in the implementation of a few methods, we may use Foq, a mocking library in the same spirit as the popular Moq for C#:

```
#r "packages/Foq/lib/net45/Foq.dll"
open Foq

let createCustomer2 (name: string) =
    Mock<ICustomer>()
        // Foq Method
        .Setup(fun x -> <@ x.HasBoughtItem(1) @>).Returns(true)
        // Foq Matching Arguments
        .Setup(fun x -> <@ x.HasBoughtItem(any()) @>).Returns(true)
```

```
// Foq Property
    .Setup(fun x -> <@ x.Name @>).Returns(name)
    .Create()
```

F# idiomatic assertions

So far, we have only seen simple assertions, such as `Assert.AreEqual`. In fact, NUnit 3 has a rich API that helps you write assertions in what almost looks like natural language:

```
Assert.That(4.99, Is.EqualTo(5.0).Within(0.05))
Assert.That(4.0, Is.Not.EqualTo(5.0).Within(0.5))
Assert.That(7, Is.GreaterThan(3))
Assert.That(7, Is.GreaterThanOrEqualTo(3))
let ints = [| 1; 2; 3; 4 |]
let strings = [| "abc"; "bad"; "cab"; "bad"; "dad" |]
CollectionAssert.AllItemsAreNotNull(ints)
CollectionAssert.AllItemsAreInstancesOfType(strings, typeof<string>)
```

This preceding kind of method feels more natural to OOP languages such as C#, however. In F#, it is usual to have curried arguments, so we can pipe the result of a previous function. It is not complicated to create some helper functions to achieve the desired effect, as follows:

```
let equals expected actual =
    Assert.AreEqual(expected, actual)

let ``Adding two plus two yields four``() =
    add 2 2
    |> equals 4
```

If we need more expressive methods, we can use the `FsUnit` library, which already contains many of these transformations of the NUnit assertions (and other .NET testing libraries such as `XUnit`) to make them more idiomatic in F#. Adding a reference to FsUnit, we can rewrite some of the previous assertions as follows:

```
#r "../packages/FsUnit/lib/net45/FsUnit.NUnit.dll"
open FsUnit

4.99 |> should (equalWithin 0.05) 5.0
4.0 |> should not' ((equalWithin 0.05) 5.0)
7 |> should greaterThan 3
7 |> should greaterThanOrEqualTo 3
```

Check the FsUnit documentation to look at the whole list of operators available.

Asynchronous tests

In C#, we need to mark a method as `async` in order to use the `await` keyword, and NUnit can automatically detect methods marked as such. In F#, we only need to use an async workflow, but unfortunately, this also means NUnit will not detect asynchronous methods in F#. We can still write asynchronous tests by using `Async.RunSynchronously`. For example, if we would like to check whether `MailboxProcessor`, an F# type to create agents (we will learn about it in the next chapter), works correctly, we could write a test as follows:

```
open System
type Message = string * AsyncReplyChannel<string>

[<Test>]
let ``MailboxProcessor.postAndAsyncReply works``() =
    async {
        let formatString = "Msg: {0} - {1}"
        let agent = MailboxProcessor<Message>.Start(fun inbox ->
            let rec loop n = async {
                let! (msg, channel) = inbox.Receive()
                do! Async.Sleep(100) // Delay a bit
                channel.Reply <|
                    String.Format(formatString, n, msg)
                if msg <> "Bye" then
                    do! loop (n + 1)
            }
            loop 0)
        let! resp = agent.PostAndAsyncReply(fun ch -> "Hi", ch)
        equals "Msg: 0 - Hi" resp
        let! resp = agent.PostAndAsyncReply(fun ch -> "Bye", ch)
        equals "Msg: 1 - Bye" resp
    }
    |> Async.RunSynchronously
```

Running NUnit tests with FAKE

So far, we have only discussed how to write tests, but it is important to also know how to run them. There are many ways to detect and run NUnit tests in Visual Studio or with GUI or console applications known as NUnit runners, but, as in F# projects we often use FAKE scripts to run builds, we will see how we can easily integrate our tests in the build process. The following is an example of a FAKE script with a target to compile and run unit tests:

```
#r "packages/FAKE/tools/FakeLib.dll"

open System
open Fake

Target "CompileAndRunTests" (fun _ ->
    // Clean and create build directory if it doesn't exist
    let buildDir = "build/tests"
    CleanDir buildDir
    CreateDir buildDir

    // COMPILE TESTS
    ["tests/MyLibTests.fsx"]
    |> FscHelper.compile [
        // F# compiler options
        FscHelper.Out (buildDir </> "MyLibTests.dll")
        FscHelper.Target FscHelper.TargetType.Library
    ]
    // Raise exception if a code other than 0 is returned
    |> function 0 -> () | c -> failwithf "Return code: %i" c
    // Copy the NUnit assembly to the build directory
    FileUtils.cp "packages/NUnit/lib/net45/nunit.framework.dll"
    buildDir

    // RUN TESTS
    [buildDir </> "MyLibTests.dll"]
    |> Testing.NUnit3.NUnit3 (fun p -> p) // Use default parameters
)

RunTargetOrDefault "CompileAndRunTests"
```

Considering the example given earlier where we write the tests in an `.fsx` script. If you had a `.fsproj` project instead, it is only necessary to change the way the tests are compiled:

```
// COMPILE TESTS
[ "tests/MyLibTests.fsproj" ]
|> MSBuildDebug buildDir "Build"
|> Log "Tests-Debug-Output: "
```

Please check the FAKE website (`http://fsharp.github.io/FAKE/`) to learn more about its capability to run common tasks in F#/C# project builds, and structure them in hierarchically dependent targets.

NUnit and Fable

In previous chapters, we introduced Fable, a tool to compile F# code into JavaScript. As Fable integrates with the JavaScript ecosystem, workflows, and tools, it is possible to write tests using any of the test frameworks available for JavaScript. However, sometimes it is interesting to write tests in the same fashion as we do for .NET–either to enable code sharing, or just because that is the way we are used to. To make this possible, there is a Fable plugin available to transform tests written for NUnit and make them compatible with **Mocha**, a popular tool for testing in JavaScript. Imagine we have a script called `FableTests.fsx`, to test that F# semantics (structural equality) work in JavaScript as well:

 Check the previous chapters to learn how to download Fable and JavaScript dependencies from npm.

```
#r "node_modules/fable-core/Fable.Core.dll"

open System
open Fable.Core
open Fable.Import

#r "packages/NUnit/lib/net45/nunit.framework.dll"
open NUnit.Framework

// If you don't want to add the NUnit dependency
// (it is not needed for JS) you can comment out
// the previous two lines and open the following namespace

// open Fable.Core.Testing

[<TestFixture>]
module MyTests =

    // Convenience method
    let equal (expected: 'T) (actual: 'T) =
        Assert.AreEqual(expected, actual)
```

```
[<Test>]
let ``Structural comparison with arrays works``() =
    let xs1 = [| 1; 2; 3 |]
    let xs2 = [| 1; 2; 3 |]
    let xs3 = [| 1; 2; 4 |]
    equal true (xs1 = xs2)
    equal false (xs1 = xs3)
    equal true (xs1 <> xs3)
    equal false (xs1 <> xs2)
```

 Note that in order to translate NUnit tests to JavaScripts with Fable, you do need to attach `TestFixtureAttribute` to the module declaration.

You can compile and run the tests in JavaScript by typing the following in the command line:

```
npm install --global fable-compiler mocha
fable FableTests.fsx --plugins node_modules/fable-plugins-
nunit/Fable.Plugins.NUnit.dll
mocha FableTests.js
```

The `Fable.Plugins.NUnit` plugin can translate the most commonly used NUnit attributes, `TestFixture` and `Test`, as well as their respective `SetUp`/`TearDown` counterparts. For assertions, however, only `Assert.AreEqual` is available at the time of writing. It is also possible to run asynchronous tests by wrapping the whole test with `async { ... } |> Async.RunSynchronously`, as in the preceding example.

Property-based testing

Unit tests are a tremendously useful tool to verify the robustness of our program. However, as we have seen in the earlier examples, we are always checking against single cases, and, even when automatically generating parameters for our tests, it is always difficult to be sure that there are no edge cases we may be missing.

The solution is not to test against the results of a function but against properties. This way, we can feed any value to the function, and verify that the properties are always fulfilled. We can also think of the properties as the requirements of the application. For example, we may want to verify that our add function, given earlier, fulfills the following three properties of addition:

- **Commutative property**: add `x` `y` should be the same as add `y` `x`

- **Associative property**: `add x y |> add z` should be the same as `add y z |> add x`

- **Identity property**: `add x 0` should be the same as `x`

Thanks to F#'s expressiveness, it is really easy to write these conditions in actually compilable code:

```
#load "MyLib.fs"

open MyLib

let addIsCommutative x y =
    add x y = add y x

let addIsAssociative x y z =
    (add x y |> add z) = (add y z |> add x)

let addHasIdentity x =
    add x 0 = x
```

Now, if we wanted to test these properties with NUnit, we would have to write three different generators for each function (as each of them takes a different number of parameters), and we would have to carefully check that the generators take all edge cases into account. `FsCheck` can do all this work for us.

```
#r "../packages/FsCheck/lib/net45/FsCheck.dll"
open FsCheck

Check.Quick addIsCommutative
Check.Quick addIsAssociative
Check.Quick addHasIdentity
```

If you run this code in F# Interactive, you should see the following result:

```
Ok, passed 100 tests.
Ok, passed 100 tests.
Ok, passed 100 tests.
```

This means that `FsCheck` has detected the number and type of parameters of each function by using reflection, automatically generated one hundred sets of parameters for each, and run them to assert that the value returned was always true.

If we want more information, we can use `Check.Verbose` instead. This will print the parameters used before each iteration.

To see how useful property-based testing can be, let's try something a bit different. Go to the `MyLib.fs` file, and modify the `add` function so that it accepts `float` instead of the inferred `int` arguments:

```
module MyLib
let add (x: float) (y: float) =
    x + y
```

Now if you try `Check.Quick addIsCommutative` again, you will get something similar to the following:

```
Falsifiable, after 13 tests (2 shrinks) (StdGen (439200737,296195468)):
Original:
nan
-11.33333333
Shrunk:
nan
11.0
```

This may be surprising: how it is possible that `int` addition is commutative, while `float` addition is not? The error message gives us a hint. In .NET, the `System.Double` type also includes `System.Double.NaN` (the value obtained by dividing 0.0 by 0.0), and in F#, *nan = nan* evaluates to false, which makes the verification fail. This may not be a showstopper for your application, but it's an example of how property-based testing can reveal unexpected results with values we don't usually take into account.

Another interesting thing we can see in the preceding output is that `FsCheck` offers us two sets of parameters: the original and the shrunk one. The former is the one that first caused the verification to fail, and the second is the minimal example that `FsCheck` could find of a failing test. The process of finding the smallest set of parameters that still causes the verification to fail is known as shrinking, and it usually provides more information to help us understand the source of the problem. In the preceding example, we can see that neither the sign nor the decimal part of `-11.33333333` is causing the problem, so we should pay closer attention to nan.

Integrating FsCheck and NUnit

It is very simple to add `FsCheck` verifications to our NUnit test suite, and is done as follows:

```
module MyLibTests

#r "../packages/NUnit/lib/net45/nunit.framework.dll"
```

```
#r "../packages/FsCheck/lib/net45/FsCheck.dll"
#load "MyLib.fs"

open MyLib
open FsCheck
open NUnit.Framework

let addIsCommutative x y =
    add x y = add y x

let addIsAssociative x y z =
    (add x y |> add z) = (add y z |> add x)

let addHasIdentity x =
    add x 0 = x

[<Test>]
    let ``Addition is additive``() =
    Check.QuickThrowOnFailure addIsCommutative

[<Test>]
let ``Addition is associative``() =
    Check.QuickThrowOnFailure addIsCommutative

[<Test>]
let ``Addition has identity``() =
    Check.QuickThrowOnFailure addIsCommutative
```

> Note that here we are using `Check.QuickThrowOnFailure` to let FsCheck throw an exception on verification failure and make the NUnit test fail.

It usually takes more time to find the properties we should verify in order to use `FsCheck`, but the robustness it ensures is difficult to achieve only with unit tests. We can streamline the process by thinking of the program properties (or business requirements) from the very design phase, and write our verifications accordingly. Also, we have seen here how to use FsCheck in the simplest way; but it is also possible to customize the generators or shrinkers if you need to. Please read the `FsCheck` documentation for more information at the following link: `https://fscheck.github.io/FsCheck/TestData.html`

Automated browser testing

Tools such as NUnit or FsCheck are very useful for testing the logic of a program, but they are not enough to check whether the user interface is working correctly. A human user is the best tester for a UI, but it is also good to automate the testing of some operations, and make sure that common tasks (such as clicking a button or opening a menu) do not crash our application. In previous chapters, we learned how to create web interfaces, not only for the browser, but also for the desktop with GitHub Electron. Now we will learn how to test our web interfaces using Canopy. According to its website, it is a web testing framework with one goal in mind: making UI testing simple.

Canopy is a self-contained application for browser UI testing providing tools not only to write tests, but also to run them. It is available in Nuget, so we can download it, for example, using Paket:

```
paket add nuget Canopy
```

 The command may vary depending on your operation system and folder structure. See Paket the documentation at the following link for more information: `https://fsprojects.github.io/Paket/paket-add.html`.

Canopy is built on top of Selenium. Selenium can interact with a number of browsers. In the case of Google Chrome, it needs a special driver that can be downloaded from `http://chromedriver.storage.googleapis.com/index.html`.

After downloading the Chrome driver, we can test our user interface with a script like the following one:

```
#r "../packages/Selenium.WebDriver/lib/net40/WebDriver.dll"
#r "../packages/canopy/lib/canopy.dll"

open canopy

// Start an instance of the Google Chrome browser
chromeDir <- "/path/to/chromedriver/"
start chrome

// This is how you define a test
"taking canopy for a spin" &&& fun _ ->

    // Go to url
    // This is a sample url available to showcase Canopy's capabilities
    url "http://lefthandedgoat.github.io/canopy/testpages/"
```

```
        // Assert that the element with an id of 'welcome' has the text
        'Welcome'
        "#welcome" == "Welcome"

        // Assert that the element with an id of 'firstName' has the value
        'John'
        "#firstName" == "John"

        // Change the value of element with an id of 'firstName' to
        'Something Else'
        "#firstName" << "Something Else"
        // Verify another element's value, click a button and verify the
        element is updated
        "#button_clicked" == "button not clicked"
        click "#button"
        "#button_clicked" == "button clicked"

    //run all tests
    run()

    // close all browsers
    quit()
```

Note that we can use CSS selectors to find elements in our page, and Canopy offers several operators to write assertions in a very expressive way (for example, use == to find an element, read its text content, and compare it with another string). There are more action and assertion helpers in Canopy, besides many settings, which we can configure to adapt the testing to our needs. Please check Canopy's website at the following link for more information: https://lefthandedgoat.github.io/canopy/actions.html.

Summary

In this chapter, you learned how to do different kinds of automated testing with F#. We started with one of the most popular techniques in .NET and other programming languages or platforms: unit testing. In F#, we can use some of the most widely used unit testing tools for .NET, such as NUnit, and benefit from its extensive functionality and compatibility with different IDEs. F# has some niceties on its own, such as having more informative names for tests and idiomatic syntax.

We then continued with property-based testing. This is not exclusive of F# or other functional programming languages, but the absence of a shared state makes it usually much easier to test properties of our functions for any given set of parameters. FsCheck makes property testing a breeze by automatically generating hundreds of samples to feed into our functions, and gives a stronger indication of robustness than simple unit tests can. FsCheck also has several tools to helps us locate problems, like shrinkers, which look for the minimal set of parameters that make our verifications fail.

Finally, you learned how to extend automated testing to the UI, thanks to Canopy. This library provides a DSL to automate common user interactions, like clicking buttons or dragging elements, and check that they produce the expected results. In the next chapter, we will take the asynchronous capabilities of F# to the next level, and learn how to write distributed programs in F#, which can run concurrently on different machines.

10
Distributed Programming in F#

"Free lunch is over" is a sentence we've been hearing in the last years about the evolution of CPU computing. Until very recently, without any effort on our end, the simple passage of time made our programs faster, thanks to the continuous improvements in the speed of computer processors. However, this is not happening any longer; CPUs are not getting faster, devices (be it a workstation, a laptop, or a mobile device) are getting more processing units instead. For developers, this means their programs won't run any faster on better machines unless they do their homework first: that is, prepare their software so it can scale up and run on multiple CPU cores in parallel. What's more, in the age of cloud computing, software also needs to scale out–run on multiple machines, overcoming problems such as corruption of shared state, locks due to race conditions, and fail recovery.

One of the reasons for the resurgence of functional programming (which, we must remember, is actually older than OOP) is precisely the advantages of this paradigm for distributed applications. Immutability solves many of the situations that lead to memory corruption or race conditions in imperative programming. Likewise, many of the functional techniques such as **MapReduce**, are a perfect fit for dividing computing tasks into independent units of work that can be easily distributed among different cores or computers. As a functional programming language, F# and its ecosystem counts as one of the many tools to help us build distributed applications that scale.

Some of the tools that help us with distributed programming in the F# ecosystem are:

- **MailboxProcessor**: Even if immutability prevents many of the problems in distributed programming, sometimes, it's unavoidable to share state between concurrent jobs. To solve this, you will learn about the Actor Model. Popularized by the Erlang language with great success for building highly available and fault-tolerant concurrent systems, the Actor Model can be implemented out of the box in F# with the built-in `MailboxProcessor` type.

- **Akka.NET**: When our application grows bigger and is deployed in the cloud, we need a more comprehensive library that allows us to implement the Actor Model on multiple machines. The Akka.NET library is a port of the popular Akka framework in the **Java Virtual Machine** (**JVM**), which includes a specific API for F#.
- **MBrace**: Sometimes, we don't need an application that is always online, but we can still make good use of distributed programming. For example, data science tasks require a lot of computing power, and the way to avoid the need to buying a huge (and expensive) workstation is to rent a computer cluster to a cloud service like Azure just for the time required to make the computations. MBrace is a library that does all the work of uploading and distributing our code in a computer cluster for us. It even makes it possible for us to use an interactive scripting environment such as the **F# Interactive** while both the data and the code to analyze live and run in the cloud. MBrace will not be covered in this chapter, but you can consult the documentation and tutorials in its website: `http://mbrace.io/`.

Actor Model

The concept of the actor programming model is very simple–our program components can be decoupled by replacing direct function calls with asynchronous messages. Different implementations of the Actor Model add other features around this idea, but at minimum, the decoupled components (the actors) include a message queue, which is thread-safe and acts as a buffer if messages come faster than the actor can process them. This is how the F# `MailboxProcessor` works.

MailboxProcessor

The `MailboxProcessor` class in the `FSharp.Core` library is used to build concurrent actors. It has some limitations, such as not being able to do interprocess communication or to persist messages in the queue in case our application crashes. But it is a very good way to easily include actors in our F# program without any additional dependencies.

As an exercise, we are going to build a dummy chat application, which includes a couple of bot users generating random messages and a human user, you. Let's create a file named `Chat.fsx`, and write the following:

```
open System
open System.Collections.Generic
```

```
type Actor<'T> = MailboxProcessor<'T>

type UserMsg =
  | Talk of author: string * message: string
  | Enter of name: string * Actor<AdminMsg>
  | Leave of name: string

and AdminMsg =
  | Message of author: string * message: string
  | AllowEntry
  | Expel
```

In the preceding code, we have opened a couple of namespaces and used a type alias to make typing MailboxProcessor a bit more pleasant. Then we defined the two types of messages we are going to use–one for chat users, and the other for the chat administrator.

We continue by creating the actor filling the role of the chat administrator, as follows:

```
let admin = Actor<UserMsg>.Start(fun actor ->
  // Keep the list of users in the chat room
  let users = Dictionary<string, Actor<AdminMsg>>()
  // ...and use a function helper to post a message to all of them
  let post msg = for u in users.Values do u.Post(msg)

  // Use an asynchronous recursive to represent the non-blocking loop
  let rec messageLoop() = async {
      let! msg = actor.Receive() // Wait until a message comes
      match msg with
      | Enter (name, actorRef) ->
          // For simplicity, just ignore duplicated users
          if users.ContainsKey name |> not then
              let msg = sprintf "User %s entered the room" name
              post <| Message("Admin", msg)
              users.Add(name, actorRef)
              actorRef.Post(AllowEntry)
      | Leave name ->
          if users.Remove(name) then
              let msg = sprintf "User %s left the room" name
              post <| Message("Admin", msg)
      | Talk(author, txt) ->
          post <| Message(author, txt)
      return! messageLoop() // Loop to top
    }

  messageLoop() // Fire up the loop
)
```

Note that the generic argument of the admin actor is `UserMsg`. This may seem contradictory, but it makes sense if you think about it, as the admin actor will receive messages from chat users and vice versa. The `MailboxProcessor.Start` method accepts a function containing the behavior of the actor with a single argument, which is, precisely, the newly created actor.

Usually, the body of the function defining the actor behavior contains a non-blocking loop (expressed here with an asynchronous recursive function) to keep the actor alive while processing new messages. Thanks to the message type being defined as a discriminated union, we can use pattern matching to tell different messages apart and react accordingly.

As you can see, the job of our chat administrator is very simple–just check that no user with the same name as that of one of the current users enters the room, and transmit messages to the rest of the users. Now we will write a function to create random users, as follows:

```
type UserState = OutOfTheRoom | InTheRoom | WaitingApproval

let makeRandomUser name sentences =
  Actor.Start(fun actor ->
    let rnd = System.Random()
    let sentencesLength = List.length sentences

    let rec messageLoop (state: UserState) = async {
      let! state = async {
        try
            let! msg = actor.Receive(timeout=rnd.Next(4000))
            match msg with
            // Ignore messages from other users
            | Message _ -> return state
            | AllowEntry -> return InTheRoom
            | Expel -> return OutOfTheRoom
        with
        | :? TimeoutException ->
            match state with
            | InTheRoom ->
              // Pick a random sentence or leave the room
              match rnd.Next(sentencesLength + 1) with
              | i when i < sentencesLength ->
                admin.Post(Talk(name, sentences.[i]))
                return state
              | _ ->
                admin.Post(Leave name)
                return OutOfTheRoom
            | OutOfTheRoom ->
              admin.Post(Enter(name, actor))
              return WaitingApproval
```

```
                | WaitingApproval ->
                    return state // Do nothing, just keep waiting
          }
        return! messageLoop state
      }
      // Start the loop with initial state
      messageLoop OutOfTheRoom
    )
```

We start defining the state of the user, which is just being out or inside the chat room, or waiting for entry approval. This last state is very important when dealing with actors–as message passing is normally asynchronous, very often, actors should be put in a transitional state until they receive a confirmation from another actor.

It could be possible to keep the state of the user in a reference cell, for example. However, here we are using a technique that is commonly used together with recursion in functional programming–state parametrization. Instead of keeping a mutable variable to store the state, we pass the updated state as a parameter to the next call to the recursive function.

As this is a very simple example, we just simulate the behavior of a real user by waiting for messages for a random time between zero and four seconds, and if nothing is received (in which case `TimeOutException` will be thrown), letting the user generate a reaction of its own.

With this helper, we can create two random users–the cheerful `Sarah` and the depressing `John`:

```
let randomUser1 =
    makeRandomUser "Sarah" [
        "Hi everybody!"
        "It feels great to be here!"
        "I missed you all so much!"
        "I couldn't agree more with that."
        "Oh, just look at the time! I should be leaving..."
    ]
let randomUser2 =
    makeRandomUser "John" [
        "Hmm, I didn't expect YOU to be here."
        "I must say, I don't feel very comfortable."
        "Is this room always so boring?"
        "I shouldn't be losing my time here."
    ]
```

Now it is time to deal with the star of the show, the human user! We will be using the console to read the human user messages, and also to print the interventions from other users, so we need to extend the `AdminMsg` type to include messages that allow the actor to interact with the console. And because the admin actor won't accept actor references different than `Actor<AdminMsg>`, we will create a middle agent to exchange messages between our human user and the admin:

```fsharp
type HumanMsg =
    | Input of string
    | Output of AsyncReplyChannel<string[]>
    | AdminMsg of AdminMsg

let humanUser =
    printf "Type your name: "
    let name = Console.ReadLine()
    let msgs = ResizeArray()
    let humanUser = Actor.Start(fun actor ->
      let rec messageLoop() = async {
          let! msg = actor.Receive()
          match msg with
          | Input txt -> admin.Post(Talk(name, txt))
          | Output reply ->
              let msgsCopy = msgs.ToArray()
              msgs.Clear()
              reply.Reply(msgsCopy)
          | AdminMsg(Message(author, txt)) ->
              sprintf "%-8s> %s" author txt |> msgs.Add
          | _ -> () // Ignore other messages for the human user
          return! messageLoop()
      }
      messageLoop()
    )
    let middleAgent = Actor.Start(fun actor ->
      let rec messageLoop() = async {
          let! msg = actor.Receive()
          humanUser.Post(AdminMsg msg)
          return! messageLoop()
      }
      messageLoop()
    )
    // Put the human user (actually, the middle agent)
    // directly in the room

    admin.Post(Enter(name, middleAgent))
    humanUser
```

Because we cannot read and print messages directly at the same time in the console (at least not without messing up user input and output), the human user actor will store the received messages until we ask to release them. Note the `Output` message ports `AsyncReplyChannel` class through which the receiver can directly send a response. This is fine for this simple example where we directly interact with the console, but normally, we should avoid this pattern, as it erases decoupling among actors and depending on the implementation, can also have an effect on performance.

Let's finish with one more loop to read and write messages in the system console:

```
let rec consoleLoop(): Async<unit> = async {
    printf "> "
    let txt = Console.ReadLine()
    if System.String.IsNullOrWhiteSpace(txt) |> not then
        humanUser.Post(Input txt)
    // Wait a bit to receive your own messafe from the admin
    do! Async.Sleep 200
    // Get the messages stored by the humanUser actor
    let! msgs = humanUser.PostAndAsyncReply
    (fun ch -> Output ch)
    msgs |> Array.iter (printfn "%s")
    return! consoleLoop()
}
printfn "Type a message to send it to the chat."
printfn @"Leave the line blank to ""pass your turn""."
consoleLoop() |> Async.RunSynchronously
```

As this last script requires interaction, it is better to run it directly from the console. Open a terminal window in the same directory where `Chat.fsx` file is located, and type the following command script:

fsi Chat.fsx

Depending on your system, you may need to write `fsharpi Chat.fsx` instead.

As an exercise, you can try to implement a user interface for the chat, and confirm that, effectively, all members (either a bot or human) are talking concurrently. This simple application shows us the advantages of the Actor Model:

- **Actors are isolated**: Thanks to this, actors can keep an internal state, which is perfectly encapsulated, as it remains invisible for other parts of our application.
- **Actors are thread-safe:** As we used an async workflow for the internal loop of the actors, the .NET task scheduler takes care that the job performed by an actor does not block other threads. At the same time, the mailbox of each actor makes it transparent to us where the message is coming from, so we don't need to worry about synchronizing threads when reacting to them.
- **Actors are decoupled**: In our case, for example, the only signature the chat administrator needs to know about the chat members is `Actor<AdminMsg>`. This allows the use of different implementations for the actors without having to change the code used by the administrator to handle the messages coming from them. In some cases, we can even use a middle agent as we did for our human actor.

The `MailboxProcessor` class is a very good way to start using the Actor Model in our application without having to add extra dependencies. However, as our system grows, we need a more comprehensive library–Akka.NET brings in many of the features missing in `MailboxProcessor`.

Akka.NET

The Akka.NET library is a port of the popular Akka framework for the JVM to the .NET platform. One of the key differences, with a more simpler implementation of the Actor Model such as `MailboxProcessor`, is that Akka.NET is distributed by default–the location of the actor remains transparent to the developer. This means that message passing will work the same locally (on the same machine) as remotely (between different machines). This makes it much easier to scale our applications without having to worry about a very complicated distribution model from the very beginning.

Another very important feature introduced by Akka is the concept of supervision–actors must be arranged in a hierarchy, with each actor being responsible for dealing with the failures causing its children actors to crash, and stopping or restarting them accordingly. This architecture helps us design highly fault-tolerant systems that can self-heal.

Let's see how we can implement the aforementioned sample using Akka actors instead of `MailboxProcessor`. As mentioned previously, let's start defining our message types as follows:

```
open Akka.Actor
open Akka.FSharp

open System
open System.Collections.Generic

type AdminMsg =
    | Talk of author: string * message: string
    | Enter of name: string * IActorRef
    | Leave of name: string

and UserMsg =
    | Message of author: string * message: string
    | AllowEntry
    | Expel

let actorSystem =
    Configuration.defaultConfig()
    |> System.create "my-system"
```

This is the same as before, except for the actor reference type (`IActorRef`), for the need of instantiating, and for the actor system that will spawn our actors. In this case, we will use the default configuration, but we will see later how we can change this.

Now we will create the actor representing the administrator of the chat:

```
let admin = spawn actorSystem "chat-admin" (fun mailbox ->
    let users = Dictionary<string, IActorRef>()
    let post msg = for u in users.Values do u <! msg
    let rec messageLoop() = actor {
        let! msg = mailbox.Receive()
        match msg with
        | Enter (name, actorRef) ->
            if users.ContainsKey name |> not then
                let msg = sprintf "User %s entered the room" name
                post <| Message("Admin", msg)
                users.Add(name, actorRef)
                actorRef <! AllowEntry
        | Leave name ->
            if users.Remove(name) then
                let msg = sprintf "User %s left the room" name
                post <| Message("Admin", msg)
```

```
                    | Talk(author, txt) ->
                        post <| Message(author, txt)
                    return! messageLoop()
            }
            messageLoop())
```

Again, the preceding code is really similar to the sample given earlier. The main differences are the function used to spawn the actor that relies on the actor system created previously and the `actor` computation expression used instead of `async`. Besides that, the lambda passed to the spawn function is practically identical to what we saw with `MailboxProcessor`–it receives a self-reference of the actor (or mailbox), and starts a recursive function that must call itself after dealing with each message to keep the actor alive.

Note that we use the tell operator (`<!`) to send messages to the actor references.

For the random users, we just need to do similar changes. Actor references (`IActorRef`) are not strongly typed in Akka, so we do not need the middle agent this time:

```
type UserState = OutOfTheRoom | InTheRoom | WaitingApproval

type RandomIntervention = RandomIntervention

let makeRandomUser name sentences =
    spawn actorSystem ("chat-member-"+name) (fun mailbox ->
        let rnd = System.Random()
        let sentencesLength = List.length sentences

        let rec msgGenerator() = async {
            do! rnd.Next(4000) |> Async.Sleep
            mailbox.Self <! RandomIntervention
            return! msgGenerator()
        }
        msgGenerator() |> Async.Start

        let rec messageLoop (state: UserState) = actor {
            let! msg = mailbox.Receive()
            // As the message is untyped, we have to do
            // some type testing first.
            match msg: obj with
            | :? UserMsg as msg ->
                match msg with
```

```
                    // Ignore messages from other users
                    | Message _ -> return! messageLoop state
                    | AllowEntry -> return! messageLoop InTheRoom
                    | Expel -> return! messageLoop OutOfTheRoom
                | :? RandomIntervention ->
                    match state with
                    | InTheRoom ->
                        // Pick a random sentence or leave the room
                        match rnd.Next(sentencesLength + 1) with
                        | i when i < sentencesLength ->
                            admin <! Talk(name, sentences.[i])
                            return! messageLoop state
                        | _ ->
                            admin <! Leave name
                            return! messageLoop OutOfTheRoom
                    | OutOfTheRoom ->
                        admin <! Enter(name, mailbox.Self)
                        return! messageLoop WaitingApproval
                    | WaitingApproval ->
                        return! messageLoop state
                         // Do nothing, just keep waiting
                | _ -> ()
        }
        // Start the loop with initial state
        messageLoop OutOfTheRoom
    )
```

 We can generate random users, passing a name and a list of sentences to the makeRandomUser expression, as previously mentioned.

And likewise, we make the following changes for the human user:

```
type HumanMsg =
    | Input of string
    | Output

let makeHumanUser name =
    spawn actorSystem "chat-member-human" (fun mailbox ->
        let msgs = ResizeArray()
        let rec messageLoop() = actor {
            let! msg = mailbox.Receive()
            match msg: obj with
            | :? HumanMsg as msg ->
                match msg with
                | Input txt -> admin <! Talk(name, txt)
```

```
                        | Output ->
                            let msgsCopy = msgs.ToArray()
                            msgs.Clear()
                            let sender = mailbox.Sender()
                            sender <! msgsCopy
                    | :? UserMsg as msg ->
                        match msg with
                        | Message(author, txt) ->
                            sprintf "%-8s> %s" author txt |> msgs.Add
                        | _ -> ()
                        // Ignore other messages for the human UserMsg
                    | _ -> ()
                    return! messageLoop()
                }
            admin <! Enter(name, mailbox.Self)
            messageLoop()
        )
```

Now we can run the sample using exactly the same code that we used for
MailboxProcessor. Only the operators used to send messages to humanUser are different:

```
[<EntryPoint>]
let main argv =
    printf "Type your name: "
    let name = Console.ReadLine()
    let humanUser = makeHumanUser name
    let rec consoleLoop(): Async<unit> = async {
        printf "> "
        let txt = Console.ReadLine()
        if System.String.IsNullOrWhiteSpace(txt) |> not then
            humanUser <! HumanMsg.Input txt
        // Wait a bit to receive your own messafe from the admin
        do! Async.Sleep 200
        // Get the messages stored by the humanUser actor
        let! msgs = humanUser <? HumanMsg.Output
        msgs |> Array.iter (printfn "%s")
        return! consoleLoop()
    }
    printfn "Type a message to send it to the chat."
    printfn @"Leave the line blank to ""pass your turn""."
    consoleLoop() |> Async.RunSynchronously
    0 // return an integer exit code
```

In the preceding code, we use the ask operator (<?) to get the output messages from `humanUser`. The ask operator returns an asynchronous operation, which can be awaited to get the message. Again, it's advised not to rely too much on this operator in spite of its usefulness, as it is much less performant than tell operations. When designing actor systems, we must prepare them for the eventuality that some messages get lost (Akka only provides an *at-most-once-delivery* guarantee) instead of eagerly waiting for a reply.

As you can see, since `MailboxProcessor` and the Akka F# API share the same concepts, once we understand how to create and communicate actors, it is very easy to write code targeting one implementation or the other.

Of course, replacing `MailboxProcessor` with Akka would be meaningless if the latter wouldn't have more features that the former. Fortunately, this is actually the case, and we will quickly overview some of the fundamentals of Akka that give it most of its power, and are not covered by `MailboxProcessor`.

Supervision

For simplicity, in the previous examples, we have put all actors at the same level. However, this is not the standard way of designing an actor system in Akka, where we must build a hierarchy instead. The reason for that is to make every actor the **supervisor** of its children. Supervision is the ground of the Erlang-inspired *let-it-crash* philosophy and frees us from having to micromanage potential exceptions throughout our whole code base. Just by stating the supervision strategy (resume, stop, restart, or escalate), each actor will react accordingly when one of its children fails.

Let's rewrite the Akka sample to create a supervisor for the random users, which will now fail from time to time. With a few changes in our code, we will see how the supervisor automatically resumes, or heals, the failing actors, improving by a great degree the robustness and availability of our system. In fact, the only part we need to modify is the code to create random users:

```
// Define a custom exception that will be thrown by random users.
// F# exceptions are easier to declare and can be pattern matched.
exception UserException of name: string

let makeRandomUser supervisor name sentences =
  spawn supervisor ("chat-member-"+name) (fun mailbox ->
    let rnd = System.Random()
    let sentencesLength = List.length sentences
```

```
let rec msgGenerator() = async {
    do! rnd.Next(4000) |> Async.Sleep
    mailbox.Self <! RandomIntervention
    return! msgGenerator()
}
msgGenerator() |> Async.Start
 let rec messageLoop (state: UserState) = actor {
    let! msg = mailbox.Receive()
    match msg: obj with
    | :? UserMsg as msg ->
        match msg with
        | Message _ -> return! messageLoop state
        | AllowEntry -> return! messageLoop InTheRoom
        | Expel -> return! messageLoop OutOfTheRoom
    | :? RandomIntervention ->
        match state with
        | InTheRoom ->
            match rnd.Next(sentencesLength + 2) with
            | i when i < sentencesLength ->
                admin <! Talk(name, sentences.[i])
                return! messageLoop state
            | i when i = sentencesLength ->
                UserException name |> raise // Throw the exception
            | _ ->
                admin <! Leave name
                return! messageLoop OutOfTheRoom
        | OutOfTheRoom ->
            admin <! Enter(name, mailbox.Self)
            return! messageLoop WaitingApproval
        | WaitingApproval ->
            return! messageLoop state
    | _ -> ()
}
messageLoop OutOfTheRoom
)
```

We only had to make two changes in the last code. First, instead of spawning the actor directly from the actor system, we pass another actor reference (actually, an IActorRefFactory interface), which will become the parent or supervisor of the new actor. Then, when generating a random intervention, we include a new case to mock a system fail and throw a custom exception.

After that, we will not create random users directly as we did previously, but a supervisor that will spawn the children on its own:

```
let randomUserSupervisor =
```

```
spawnOpt actorSystem "random-user-supervisor"
    <| fun mailbox ->
        let randomUser1 =
            makeRandomUser mailbox "Sarah" sarahSentences
        let randomUser2 =
            makeRandomUser mailbox "John" johnSentences
        let rec messageLoop() = actor {
            let! msg = mailbox.Receive()
            // Do nothing as this supervisor won't
            // receive messages.
            // In the case we need to forward the
            // message to a child,
            // we can use Forward, as in `randomUser1.Forward(msg)`
            return! messageLoop()
        }
        messageLoop()
    <| [ SupervisorStrategy(
            Strategy.OneForOne(function
            | UserException name ->
                printfn "Resuming %s..." name
                Directive.Resume
            | _ -> Directive.Escalate)) ]
```

In the preceding code, instead of the spawn function, we use spawnOpt, which also accepts a list of options. The option list comes at the end, and in this case, it just contains a supervisor strategy. There are two possible strategies:

- **one-for-one**: This is the default strategy that will apply the directive to the failing actor
- **one-for-all**: This will also apply it to its siblings. This strategy is useful when actors in the same group have tight dependencies, so corruption of the state in one of them requires restarting all the other actors as well.

The strategy accepts one argument–a decider, a function that receives the raised exception and returns a directive, the way to respond to the failure. As commented earlier, this can either be restarting, resuming, or stopping the actor on one hand, or escalating the problem to the upper supervision level on the other. In our case, we react to our custom exception by resuming the actor or escalating the problem for other types of exceptions.

Strategies can also accept other arguments besides the decider, such as timeout or the number of possible retries. Please refer to the Akka.NET documentation for details.

Note that the strategy does not accept the identity of the failing child. This is intended as an incentive to create actor groups according to healing strategies. When you need different strategies to deal with different problems, a new level of supervision must be added.

With these modifications, we can run the code, and we will see the same behavior as in the previous example. This time, the random users will fail on occasion but will be resumed by the supervisor, preventing the system from failing completely.

An important point to take into consideration is that the supervision hierarchy doesn't correspond to the hierarchy of our domain model. In this example, this means the administrator cannot act as the supervisor of the chat members. This is because the supervisor cannot change the state of its children if they are exchanging messages. (The supervisor can forward messages to its children, though.)

Supervision is a very powerful concept, but what really makes Akka much more powerful than `MailboxProcessor` is the possibility of deploying and communicating with actors in remote machines. We will see now how we can make our chat members communicate through a network.

Remote actors

Akka is distributed by default. This means that actors will work the same no matter whether they are deployed on the same or remote machines. In fact, if in our previous examples the actors were deployed on different machines, we would only need very few changes to the existing code to make them communicate. Another powerful feature is **remote deployment**, which allows us to write the code for one actor in one machine and effectively deploy it in another through another machine. This makes it possible to extend the functionality of a system without restarting, which is a necessary characteristic of highly available systems.

To illustrate this, we are going to modify our chat example to make it work on two different machines. For that purpose, we have to split the code into two different projects. First, we will deal with the code that will run on a remote machine. Akka makes remote communication almost transparent to the user, but there are a couple of things we need to be aware of–while it is possible to share assemblies, to prevent tight-coupling between remote systems, we will only use primitive messages for easier serialization. Because of this, we will start writing a couple of helper functions that help us transform back and forth between union types and primitive values back and forth:

```
open FSharp.Reflection
```

```
/// Active pattern to recognize both unions
/// or serialized (string * obj list) tuples
let (|TryUnion|_|) (x: obj): 'T option =
    match x with
    | null -> None
    | :? 'T as x -> Some x
    | :? (string*obj list) as union ->
        try
            let case, fields = union
            FSharpType.GetUnionCases(typeof<'T>)
            |> Seq.tryFind (fun uci -> uci.Name = case)
            |> Option.map (fun uci ->
                FSharpValue.MakeUnion(uci, List.toArray fields)
                |> unbox<'T>)
        with _ -> None
    | _ -> None

/// Helper function to convert a union in a tuple
/// that can be serialized and send remotely
let tuple (u: obj) =
    let uci, fields = FSharpValue.GetUnionFields(u, u.GetType())
    uci.Name, List.ofArray fields
```

With a little bit of F# reflection, we wrote an active pattern (TryUnion), which can be used with pattern matching, and accepts two types of messages:

- **Typed unions**: A actors in the same system can directly send a typed union, because they share the same code base.
- **(string * obj list) tuples**: Representing the case name and the fields of a union type. This makes it really easy to serialize messages without the need of any external library.

Likewise, we have another function that extracts the case name and the fields of a union type, and converts it into a tuple.

The next thing we need is a configuration. The previous examples were simple enough for the default settings, but when dealing with remote actors, we need some configuration. Akka.NET uses the HOCON format for that–a JSON superset designed to be more human-readable (you can check the HOCON repository on GitHub for more information). Usually, this configuration will go in a separate file (or maybe embedded in App.config), but for simplicity, here we will write it directly in our code:

```
open Akka.FSharp
open Akka.Actor
open System.Collections.Generic
```

```
// When testing remotely, write the IP of **this system**
// instead of `localhost`
let config = Configuration.parse """
akka {
    actor {
        provider = "Akka.Remote.RemoteActorRefProvider, Akka.Remote"
    }
    remote.helios.tcp {
        transport-protocol = tcp
        hostname = localhost
        port = 7000
    }
}
"""
```

 Although it is not necessary to open a specific namespace, we need to add the Akka.Remote NuGet package to our project in order to use Akka remote workers.

To make it easier to test the project, the configuration assumes that you are running both programs (the remote and local parts) on the same machine, but you can easily run them on different machines by replacing localhost in the configuration with the proper IP address, as specified in the comment.

This project will create the admin and random users actors, so we start with the following function:

```
type AdminMsg =
    | Talk of author: string * message: string
    | Enter of name: string * IActorRef
    | Leave of name: string

and UserMsg =
    | Message of author: string * message: string
    | AllowEntry
    | Expel

let makeAdmin system =
    spawn system "chat-admin" (fun mailbox ->
        let users = Dictionary<string, IActorRef>()
        let post msg = for u in users.Values do u <! msg
        let rec messageLoop() = actor {
            let! msg = mailbox.Receive()
            match msg: obj with
            | TryUnion (msg: AdminMsg) ->
                match msg with
```

```
        | Enter (name, actorRef) ->
            if users.ContainsKey name |> not
            then
                let msg =
                    sprintf "User %s entered the room" name
                post <| Message("Admin", msg)
                users.Add(name, actorRef)
                actorRef <! tuple AllowEntry
                msg
            else sprintf "User %s is already in the room" name
        | Leave name ->
            if users.Remove(name)
            then
                let msg = sprintf "User %s left the room" name
                post <| Message("Admin", msg)
                msg
            else sprintf "User %s was not in the room" name
        | Talk(author, txt) ->
            post <| tuple (Message (author, txt))
            sprintf "%-8s> %s" author txt
        |> printfn "%s"
    | _ ->
        printfn "Unknown message received"
    return! messageLoop()
  }
  messageLoop())
```

In the preceding function's code, we started with the definition of the union types to represent the messages. As you have probably noticed, they are identical to the previous examples, because the field types of all cases are serializable in Akka, including actor references.

With a few differences, the code to create the admin actor is also very similar to the previous examples. The main difference is that now we have to deal with messages as typed unions (from actors on the same machine) or tuples (from remote actors), so we use the previously defined `TryUnion` active pattern instead of matching the union type directly. Likewise, before posting to the actors, we use the `tuple` function to make sure that the message is serializable through a network. Also, because now the user input will come from another machine, the admin can directly print the messages without worrying about terminal pollution.

Now it's the turn of the random users:

```
type UserState = OutOfTheRoom | InTheRoom | WaitingApproval

type RandomIntervention = RandomIntervention
```

```
let makeRandomUser system (admin: IActorRef) name sentences =
  spawn system ("chat-member-"+name) (fun mailbox ->
    let rnd = System.Random()
    let sentencesLength = List.length sentences
    let rec msgGenerator() = async {
        do! rnd.Next(4000) |> Async.Sleep
        mailbox.Self <! RandomIntervention
        return! msgGenerator()
    }
    msgGenerator() |> Async.Start
    let rec messageLoop (state: UserState) = actor {
        let! msg = mailbox.Receive()
        match msg: obj with
        | TryUnion (msg: UserMsg) ->
            match msg with
            | Message _ -> return! messageLoop state
            | AllowEntry -> return! messageLoop InTheRoom
            | Expel -> return! messageLoop OutOfTheRoom
        | TryUnion (_: RandomIntervention) ->
            match state with
            | InTheRoom ->
                match rnd.Next(sentencesLength + 1) with
                | i when i < sentencesLength ->
                    admin <! Talk(name, sentences.[i])
                    return! messageLoop state
                | _ ->
                    admin <! Leave name
                    return! messageLoop OutOfTheRoom
            | OutOfTheRoom ->
                admin <! Enter(name, mailbox.Self)
                return! messageLoop WaitingApproval
            | WaitingApproval ->
                return! messageLoop state
        | _ -> ()
    }
    messageLoop OutOfTheRoom
)
```

Again, the only difference with the previous examples is that we use the `TryUnion` active pattern to be able to recognize local and remote messages.

As commented, this project won't create the actor for the human user, so we can directly write the code to start the chat, as follows:

```
[<EntryPoint>]
let main _ =
    // The remote system only listens for incoming connections.
```

```
// It will receive actor creation request from local-system.
use system = System.create "remote-system" config
let admin = makeAdmin system
let randomUser1 =
    makeRandomUser system admin "Sarah" sarahSentences
let randomUser2 =
    makeRandomUser system admin "John" johnSentences
System.Console.ReadLine() |> ignore
0
```

If you run the project, you will see the random users happily chatting with each other. But we want to have our say too, so we will create a different project to create an actor that handles user input, and is deployed remotely to the actor system we just fired up. Let's create a new project (also adding the Akka.FSharp and Akka.Remote packages), and start by declaring some helpers and the configuration as we did previously:

```
// Open modules in this order, as Akka.FSharp can shadow
// some members from Akka.Actor
open Akka.FSharp
open Akka.Actor

// Create remote deployment configuration from the system address
let remoteDeploy systemPath =
    let address =
        match ActorPath.TryParseAddress systemPath with
        | false, _ -> failwith "ActorPath address cannot be parsed"
        | true, a -> a
    Deploy(RemoteScope(address))

// When testing remotely, write the IP of **this system**
// instead of `localhost`
let config = Configuration.parse """
akka {
    actor.provider = ""Akka.Remote.RemoteActorRefProvider,
    Akka.Remote""
    remote.helios.tcp {
        transport-protocol = tcp
        hostname = localhost
        port = 9001
    }
}
"""

// When testing remotely, write the IP of **the remote system**
// instead of `localhost`
let [<Literal>] remoteSystemAddress =
```

```
            "akka.tcp://remote-system@localhost:7000"

    // These literal tags allow some level of safety
    // while keeping the messages serializable
    module Msg =
        let [<Literal>] Talk = "Talk"
        let [<Literal>] Enter = "Enter"
        let [<Literal>] Input = "Input"
```

As you can see, this time we need to specify the address of the remote system, as that will be the destiny of the human user actor. Also, even if we don't have access to the union types defined in the previous project, we declare some literal tags that correspond to the case names that we want to emulate.

Time to create the human user actor, and introduce several new concepts in the process:

```
    let makeHumanUser system (name: string) =
        spawne system "chat-member-human-remote"
            <@
                // Use this operator to make value boxing less verbose
                let (!) (x:obj) = box x
                fun mailbox ->
                    let admin =
                        // Select the admin actor by its path
                        let path = remoteSystemAddress + "/user/chat-admin"
                        select path mailbox.Context.System
                    let rec messageLoop(): Cont<string*obj list, unit> =
                        actor {
                            let! msg = mailbox.Receive()
                            match msg with
                            | Msg.Input, [txt] ->
                                // The message is just a tuple of a string and
                                // a list of serializable objects, which can be
                                // sent over the network without
                                // sharing any assembly.
                                admin <! (Msg.Talk, [!name; !txt])
                            | _ -> ()
                            return! messageLoop()
                        }
                    admin <! (Msg.Enter, [!name; !mailbox.Self])
                    messageLoop()
            @>
            // Serialize the code and deploy the actor in the remote system
            [ SpawnOption.Deploy(remoteDeploy remoteSystemAddress) ]
```

This actor will be deployed remotely, so we need to use the function `spawne`, which, instead of a lambda, accepts an F# quotation with code that can be sent to the remote system. To make the code fully serializable, it is very important that the quotation does not include references to types or methods in non-shared assemblies. Here, we only use types or methods belonging to the .NET base class library, `FSharp.Core`, or Akka. Messages are directly `(string * obj list)` tuples.

 Make sure all the references to string values are marked as `[<Literal>]` so that the quotation inline the value, and doesn't try to access the member in the decoupled assembly.

The human actor needs a reference to the admin actor in order to post the messages. As this is a different project, we obviously don't have direct access to the reference, but Akka lets us `select` actors by their addresses, which is what we do in this case.

Now we just need to write the code to run the program. This time, we will only accept user input, as the chat messages will be displayed on the remote terminal:

```
[<EntryPoint>]
let main _ =
    use system = System.create "local-system" config
    printf "Type your name: "
    let name = System.Console.ReadLine()
    let humanUser = makeHumanUser system name
    let rec consoleLoop(): Async<unit> = async {
        printf "> "
        let txt = System.Console.ReadLine()
        if System.String.IsNullOrWhiteSpace(txt) |> not then
            humanUser <! ("Input", [box txt])
        return! consoleLoop()
    }
    printfn "Type a message to send it to the chat."
    consoleLoop() |> Async.RunSynchronously
    0
```

If you run this code while the previous project is still running, you will see how the messages you write in the console will be displayed on the remote terminal. The human actor has been effectively deployed to the remote system, and it will be kept alive there even if you shut down the local machine.

Summary

In this chapter, we learned about the Actor Model when simple functions are not enough to express the needs of our domain model in a distributed way, the Erlang-inspired model is a very powerful tool to break our program into decoupled actors, which can asynchronously exchange messages with each other. Though limited, the `FSharp.Core` library provides `MailboxProcessor` to implement this model in our programs without any extra dependency. Later we learned about distributed actors with Akka.NET and how Akka takes the Actor Model one step beyond and allows you to communicate and deploy actors remotely. Akka also introduces the concept of supervision, which helps design highly available systems that heal themselves. Also, the `Akka.FSharp` package provides a specific API for F# making it more pleasant for developers of this language to interact with the library.

Remember also the F# language and ecosystem offer other possibilities for distributed computing, like scripting on the cloud when the power of our development machine is not enough for the most demanding tasks like machine learning or data science. In these cases, we can use MBrace to transparently upload and distribute our code in a computer cluster in the cloud, even when scripting with F# Interactive.

Index

automatic vehicle location (AVL) 59

B

balanced red-black trees 62, 63
basic values 18, 19
binary trees 60, 62
Browserify 183

C

Canopy
  about 205, 218
  reference 219
Chrome driver
  reference 218
Chromium 182
class
  defining 70
collection modules
  about 43
  Array 44, 50
  List 44, 55
  Map 44, 59
  Seq 44
  Set 44, 58
command-line interpreter (CLI) 172
Common Language Infrastructure mutable records
  33
Common Language Runtime (CLR) 7
commutative property 214
comparison operators
  about 36, 37
  attributes 38
conditions
  working with 69
constructors
  about 71
  additional constructor 71
  primary constructor 71
control structures
  about 65
  conditions 68
  loops 66
custom equality constraint
  defining 38
custom operators 25

D

delegates
  declaring 100
design patterns, with MailboxProcessor
  about 123
  agents 128
  errors 128
  functional approach, of type-safe
    MailboxProcessor 125
  imperative approach, of type-safe
    MailboxProcessor 124
  messages 126
  results, reporting from mailbox 126, 128
  union types 126
distributed programming, in F#
  Actor Model 221
  Akka.NET 222, 228, 229
  MBrace 222
DotLiquid 164

E

EF Code First approach 144
electron-prebuilt package 186
Electron
  folders 184, 185
  main process 182
  React components, using with 194, 198, 199
  renderer process 182
encapsulation 69
Entity Framework (EF) 144
equality operators
  about 37
  attributes 38
ES2015 modules, in Mozilla Developer Network
    (MDN)
  reference 196
ES6 classes
  reference 197
event processing 98, 99, 100
events
  about 96
  declaring 97, 98
explicit fields 74, 75
extensions 84

www.ingramcontent.com/pod-product-compliance
Lightning Source LLC
Chambersburg PA
CBHW060535060326
40690CB00017B/3501